STUDIES IN ENGLISH LITERATURES

Edited by Koray Melikoğlu

Rana Tekcan

Too Far For Comfort

A Study on Biographical Distance

Second, Revised and Expanded Edition

STUDIES IN ENGLISH LITERATURES

Edited by Koray Melikoğlu

ISSN 1614-4651

10 *Paola Baseotto*
"Disdeining life, desiring leaue to die"
Spenser and the Psychology of Despair
ISBN 978-3-89821-567-1

11 *Annie Gagiano*
Dealing with Evils
Essays on Writing from Africa
2nd, revised and expanded edition
ISBN 978-3-8382-0687-5

12 *Thomas F. Halloran*
James Joyce: Developing Irish Identity
A Study of the Development of Postcolonial Irish Identity in the Novels of James Joyce
ISBN 978-3-89821-571-8

13 *Pablo Armellino*
Ob-scene Spaces in Australian Narrative
An Account of the Socio-topographic Construction of Space in Australian Literature
ISBN 978-3-89821-873-3

14 *Lance Weldy*
Seeking a Felicitous Space on the Frontier
The Progression of the Modern American Woman in O. E. Rölvaag, Laura Ingalls Wilder, and Willa Cather
ISBN 978-3-89821-535-0

15 *Rana Tekcan*
Too Far For Comfort
A Study on Biographical Distance
2nd, revised and expanded edition
ISBN 978-3-89821-995-2

16 *Paola Brusasco*
Writing Within/Without/About Sri Lanka
Discourses of Cartography, History and Translation in Selected Works by Michael Ondaatje and Carl Muller
ISBN 978-3-8382-0075-0

17 *Zeynep Z. Atayurt*
Excess and Embodiment in Contemporary Women's Writing
ISBN 978-3-89821-978-5

18 *Gianluca Delfino*
Time, History, and Philosophy in the Works of Wilson Harris
ISBN 978-3-8382-0265-5

19 *Taner Can*
Magical Realism in Postcolonial British Fiction: History, Nation, and Narration
ISBN 978-3-8382-0754-4

Rana Tekcan

TOO FAR FOR COMFORT

A Study on Biographical Distance

Second, Revised and Expanded Edition

ibidem-Verlag
Stuttgart

Bibliographic information published by the Deutsche Nationalbibliothek
Die Deutsche Nationalbibliothek lists this publication in the Deutsche Nationalbibliografie; detailed bibliographic data are available in the Internet at http://dnb.d-nb.de.

Bibliografische Information der Deutschen Nationalbibliothek
Die Deutsche Nationalbibliothek verzeichnet diese Publikation in der Deutschen Nationalbibliografie; detaillierte bibliografische Daten sind im Internet über http://dnb.d-nb.de abrufbar.

Cover picture: Joshua Reynolds. Self-portrait, ca. 1748.
Source: http://commons.wikimedia.org/wiki/File:Sir_Joshua_Reynolds_012.jpg#filehistory.
Public domain.

2nd, revised and expanded edition

1st edition: The Biographer and the Subject. A Study on Biographical Distance. *ibidem* Press, Stuttgart: 2010.

ISSN: 1614-4651

ISBN-13: 978-3-8382-0735-3

Printed in the United States of America

For Ali and Lale
and for Selim

Table of Contents

Acknowledgements vii

Foreword 1

1 Eating and Drinking with the Subject:
Johnson's *Life of Savage* and Boswell's *Life of Johnson* 11

2 Judas and the Frog Prince:
Strachey's *Eminent Victorians* and Holroyd's *Lytton Strachey* 69

3 Too Far for Comfort:
Honan's *Jane Austen, Her Life* and Motion's *Keats* 113

Afterword 143

Bibliography 165

Index 177

Acknowledgements

I owe a debt of gratitude to Prof. Manuel Schonhorn of Southern Illinois University, Carbondale who introduced me to biographical studies; to Prof. Cevza Sevgen, my doctoral supervisor at Boğaziçi University, who guided me through this work; to the faculty members at Istanbul Bilgi University Comparative Literature Department who daily create the most congenial work environment any academic can wish for; to the staff at Istanbul Bilgi University Library who provided prompt and informed research support; and finally, to Koray Melikoğlu, my editor, who gave thoughtful and meticulous editorial assistance.

Parts of this book were used in a presentation, subsequently published, for the *"Life Writing" Symposium* held at Haliç University, Istanbul, 19-21 April 2006 (see bibliography).

Foreword

> To understand just one life, you have to swallow the world.
>
> Salman Rushdie, *Midnight's Children*

Biographers are curious people. Their business is other people's lives. They stand at the crossroads of human curiosity and a certain kind of generosity: By plunging into the life of another, they try to realize an individual's ultimate attempt at understanding, reconstructing, even recreating the life of another individual, at capturing the essence of a life and a mind. At the same time, by making this attempt public, they gratify the curiosity of other individuals.

Biographers have to face the daunting task of dealing with all sorts of diverse material such as letters, diaries, or interviews. Most of them visit the places where their subjects have lived, travel to where they have travelled, read what they have read. This is a way to trace imagine, and finally, to reconstruct the subject's life. The final outcome does not reflect a simple listing of discovered facts, but a series of choices specific to the rendition of the subject by the biographer. This is at the heart of the phenomenon of multiple biographies of the same subject. Each biographer imagines and recreates the subject through the available material. Since no two people interpret the same material in quite the same way, no two recreations are the same. Therefore, there are as many subjects as there are biographies of that subject. The extent of this multiplicity of biographical interpretation should be illustrated in some detail before a discussion of the narrative dynamic between the biographer and the subject is attempted.

Multiple biographies of the English novelist Jane Austen may well be used for this purpose. Since her death in 1817, Jane Austen's life has inspired quite a number of biographical writings. Austen's letters to her sister Cassandra and occasionally to other family members, memoirs, family papers, parish registers and other similar documents are among the standard sources utilized by her biographers, and no groundbreaking new material has been discovered since William Austen-Leigh and Richard Arthur Austen-Leigh published *Jane Austen, Her Life and Letters, A Family Record* in 1913.[1] Yet, since then, each of her subsequent biographers must have felt that the previous biographies lacked in certain aspects, that they somehow failed to present their subject "as she *really* was".

Deeply private and reticent by nature, Jane Austen – the much wondered about "lady" who wrote the greatly admired[2] novels – certainly did not volunteer any information on herself. The first biographical information on the author came out almost as a necessity. One of her older brothers (incidentally, her favourite), Henry Austen felt himself obliged to respond to the many inquiries about the private life of the author after her death. He added a "Biographical Notice of the Author" to the 1817 (title page 1818) posthumous joint publication of *Northanger Abbey* and *Persuasion.* In it he describes his sister in the following manner:

> Her stature was that of true elegance. It could not have been increased without exceeding the middle height. Her carriage and deportment were quiet, yet graceful. Her features were separately good. Their assemblage produced an unrivalled expression of that cheerfulness, sensibility, and benevolence, which were her real characteristics. Her complexion was of the finest texture. It might with truth be said, that her eloquent blood spoke through her modest cheek. Her voice was extremely sweet. She delivered herself with fluency and precision. Indeed she was formed for elegant and rational society, excelling in conversation as much as in composition. [...] She had not only an excellent taste for drawing, but, in earlier

[1] This work is a factual record of Austen's life. In 1989, Austen scholar Deirdre Le Faye published a revised and enlarged version titled *Jane Austen, A Family Record*, filling gaps and correcting certain errors.

[2] The Prince Regent kept copies of her novels in each of his residences.

> days, evinced great power of hand in the management of the pencil. [...] She was fond of dancing, and excelled in it. [...] Though the frailties, foibles, and follies of others could not escape her immediate detection, yet even on their vices did she never trust herself to comment with unkindness. Faultless herself, as nearly as human nature can be, she always sought, in the faults of others, something to excuse, to forgive or to forget. She never uttered either a hasty, a silly or severe expression. [...] She was thoroughly religious and devout; fearful of giving offence to God, and incapable of feeling it towards any fellow creature. (31-33)

The affectionate brother-as-biographer depicts Austen as the ideal "spinster" sister: elegant, sensible, benevolent, cheerful, dutiful, quiet, accomplished and religious. She appears to be the epitome of perfection very much in line with the norms for unmarried women at the turn of the nineteenth century. Yet, biographical research brings to light the natural fact that not everyone who knew her was so adoring. An old family friend from Hampshire, a Mrs. Milford, remembered Austen at a time when her authorship began to be known. Miss Milford, her daughter, wrote the following in a letter:

> I have discovered that our great favourite Miss Austen is my country-woman; that Mama knew all her family very intimately; and that herself is an old maid (I beg her pardon – I mean a young lady) with whom Mama before her marriage was acquainted. Mama says she was then the prettiest, silliest, most affected husband-hunting butterfly she ever remembers and a friend of mine who visits her now says that she has stiffened into the most perpendicular, precise, taciturn piece of "single blessedness" that ever existed, and that till "Pride and Prejudice" showed what a precious gem was hidden in that unbending case, she was no more regarded in society than a poker or a fire screen or any other thin, upright piece

> of wood or iron that fills its corner in peace and quiet. The case is very different now; she is still a poker but a poker of whom everyone is afraid. It must be confessed that this silent observation from such an observer is rather formidable … a wit, a delineator of character, who does not talk is terrific indeed. (W. and R. A. Austen-Leigh, rev. ed. 198-99)

Biographers need to decide what they will do with both the statement of the brother and the statement above. How are they to be reconciled? *Should* they be reconciled? One way is to ignore one of them altogether. Another is to interpret them in a way supporting the biographer's overall picture of the author that will come across in the biography. In her *Only a Novel: The Double Life of Jane Austen* (1972), Jane Aiken Hodge fits Mrs. Milford's "the prettiest, silliest, most affected husband-hunting butterfly" comment within her vision of Austen living a conforming public life on the one hand and a private creative life on the other. She keeps silent about the rest:

> I like to think that this report might have been superficially correct, though basically false […] what was intended as criticism was in fact high praise. It shows how successfully Jane Austen had embarked on her double life. Young ladies were supposed to be pretty, and silly, and on the catch for husbands. Jane Austen had decided to conform. And as "an artist can do nothing slovenly", she was naturally, the prettiest and silliest of them all. (46)

Hodge ties Mrs Mitford's statement to Austen's own statement on artistry and presents her actions as conscious social choices. Six years later another biographer, Lord David Cecil comments on the Milford letter in his *A Portrait of Jane Austen*:

> On examination these sharp words turn out to have little evidence to support them. For one thing, Mrs. Milford left the

> Steventon district when Jane was only ten years old, so that she can only be speaking on hearsay. For another, the description [...] is at variance with everything else we know about Jane Austen. Whatever false impression she may have made at twelve years old, it is incredible that the grown-up Jane Austen, the Jane Austen who, within a few years, was to create such devastating embodiments of silliness and affectation as Lucy Steele and Isabella Thorpe, should herself have ever appeared as affected, let alone silly. Or husband-hunting; though, like most girls of her age, she probably considered any young man she met in the light of a possible husband. Altogether Mrs. Milford's account must be considered mainly worthless. Personally, I should be sorry to regard it as wholly worthless. I like to think there was a time in Jane Austen's life when she could be called a pretty butterfly. I know of no other women writer of the first rank who has been similarly described. (67)

Although Cecil dismisses the document at first, he cannot keep himself from commenting on it in a way that supports his own vision of the author as a well-adjusted woman who would shun folly in any shape or form. He gives credit to the statement, in the manner of an understanding father, by making the reader imagine a livelier, true-to-life young girl who had the artistic vision as well as the social experience to write the sparkling *Pride and Prejudice*.

The theme of love and marriage is also an important concern for Austen biographers. Since her sister Cassandra burnt the letters that are commonly supposed to include these subjects, and very little else is known about the love life of one of the most successful writers of love, the biographers have to make do with what they have. It is a known fact that the son of a wealthy family friend, Harris Bigg-Wither proposed to Austen. He was accepted. However, the following morning Austen apologized and withdrew her acceptance. This change of heart – or mind – is easily accepted by female biographers. Elizabeth Jenkins, for example, simply writes, "[when] it came [...] to marrying without love, she could not do it" (102). Male biographers, on the other hand, have a harder time accepting her refusal of a wealthy man from a good family at a time in her life when it could have been a much-needed financial and social relief. Park Honan spends six pages justifying the decision and ends up almost apologizing for Austen.

Even the letters that are generally considered reliable can acquire different meanings depending on the way they are read. Austen writes to her sister Cassandra about the book she is planning to write, then says "Now I will try to write of something else, and it shall be a complete change of subject – ordination" (Chapman 298). For a long time, it was thought that Austen was referring to *Mansfield Park* in which Edmund Bertram's ordination carries great import. Scholars commented that Austen was announcing a total change of subject in her new novel, and that her primary concern was ordination. This was considered the standard interpretation. But, later on, a more careful reading of the letter and a closer attention to punctuation revealed that when Austen wrote about the change of subject, she merely meant that she was changing the subject *in her letter*, the ordination she would be writing about was not Edmund Bertram's fictional ordination, but the very factual ordination ceremony of Austen's elder brother James Austen (Honan 336). Biographical researchers can get so excited when they think that they have found new information that they may misread a text.

There are also deliberate misreadings. John Halperin, author of *The Life of Jane Austen*, seems to have started writing with an intention to bring forth a side of Austen many readers do not know existed, and many Austen scholars do not want to accept. This sensationalist approach leads to misquotations such as exchanging 'possible' for the original word 'impossible' while quoting from Henry Austen's "Biographical Notice" (Halperin 5), which reversed the meaning. Halperin wants to emphasize Austen's less than perfect relationship with her mother. He quotes from Austen's letter to Anne Sharp (Thursday, 22 May 1817) which she wrote during her last illness (344). In this letter, Austen talks about her appreciation of her sister and brothers for their kindness and care during her illness; but Halperin claims that she does not mention her mother. This is presented as proof of the coldness that existed between them even just before Austen's death. In order to prove his point, Halperin conveniently omits this sentence which comes further on in the letter: "I have not mentioned my dear Mother; she suffered much for me when I was at the worst, but is tolerably well. [...] In short, if I live to be an old Woman, I must expect to wish to die now; blessed in the tenderness of such a Family [...]" (Chapman 203). He presents Jane Austen as a bitter, sarcastic, frustrated spinster; the biography is full of words like "pettiness," "nastiness," "mean spiritedness" and "cold-hearted." This is Halperin's Austen.

Which is the *real* Austen? Maybe all or maybe none. Yet one thing is certain: There are as many Austens as there are Austen biographies, and there can be no "definitive biography" except in the blurbs that grace the covers of biographies themselves.

This brief look at the roots of the elusiveness of the subject in biography as a genre reveals that the earlier statement – that there are as many subjects as there are biographies – can be reworded in a way that would put the issue more accurately: there are as many subjects as there are biographers. Access to biographical material is an important factor in the differences between biographies; nevertheless, given exactly the same material to work with, no two biographers will draw the same conclusions. Therefore, the key is the interpretation of the biographer. After all, each attempt at writing the life of a subject is unique in that each carries the imprint of the interpretive and creative faculties of a biographer's mind.

The main interest of this book is the various ways of recreating the "biographical self" in narrative, in other words, the intricate relationship of the biographer with the subject. What exactly does a biographer do when s/he gives shape to a life in a biography? This is a question widely ignored both by readers and reviewers of biography. Most reviews of biographies in literary magazines and journals – and there are many, since biography is a highly popular genre – ignore the narrative strategies and styles of the biographies as if they were directly looking at the content. But what is content without form? It is biographical form that gives shape to the biographical subject. Without it no illusion of a living and breathing person can be created on paper. The recreation of the biographical subject is a complex endeavour and requires a complex narrative. In contrast to purely fictional forms, biography writing does not allow total freedom to the biographer in the creative act. Ideally, a biography's structure or backbone is formed by accurate historical fact – in that sense, it claims a kinship with history. But its soul lies elsewhere. Since the concern is life, something more is needed. This "something more" is desired both by writers and readers of biography: It is the vivid sense of a lived life; nothing dry, cold or dead, but a well-rounded, vibrant impression of a life that is left in the air after one turns over the last page of a biography of literary value.

Each biographer uses different narrative strategies to create this impression; however, s/he is, once again, unable to exercise total freedom. The use of these narrative strategies cannot be arbitrary. It is dictated by what will be called the "distance" between the biographer and the subject in terms of time and space (Alpers 12). Distance serves as a centre around which the issues of biographer and subject relationship can be discussed. Looking at biography in terms of distance also enables us to divide this diverse genre into three main categories for closer analysis.

In the first category, the distance is close – almost non-existent. The biographer is personally acquainted with the subject and writes the biography either at the time when the subject is alive or not much later than his/her death. In most of these cases the biographers are relatives or close friends of the subject. No matter who they are, they have firsthand knowledge of their subjects and more often than not, have access to personal documents. Many biographers and readers consider such an acquaintance as an advantage, yet "its accompanying liability of nearly unavoidable bias has almost as often been viewed as a challenge, sometimes even an outright obstacle, to the modern ideal of skeptical objectivity" (Parke 4).

The biographers in the second group are near contemporaries of their subjects. Although they do not know them personally, they "either possess, or [are] equipped to acquire, a thorough understanding of the [...] subject's background and sphere of activities" (Alpers 12).

The biographers in the final category are distinctly removed from their subjects. Let alone knowing them personally, some of them do not even have a chance to know what their subjects look like. Although this might seem like a disadvantage, in certain cases it might actually be a blessing in disguise. Safely removed from the subjects as well as their close relatives and friends, sometimes by hundreds of years, these biographers enjoy a kind of creative freedom away from the watchful eyes of fierce protectors of biographical material whom biographers from the other two categories sometimes have to fight against.

Two biographies from each category are selected for this study. The purpose is firstly, to do at least some justice to the immense variety of the genre; secondly, and more importantly, to illustrate how the approach to the subject and the employment of narrative strategies may vary under similar circumstances. It will be noted that five out of these six biographies are literary biographies in the sense that they are biographies of literary figures. This selection is not deliberate, since the book will not concern itself with any specific or common attribute of the subjects themselves. What is deliberate though is that they all satisfy the second definition of the term: They all are biographies of considerable literary quality.

1 Eating and Drinking with the Subject: Johnson's *Life of Savage* and Boswell's *Life of Johnson*

> Nobody can write the life of a man, but those who have eat and drunk and lived in social intercourse with him.
>
> Samuel Johnson, *The Life of Samuel Johnson LL.D.*

There is a group of biographers who are historically placed at such a privileged moment that they are able to see their subjects with their own eyes. Does it follow that the strongest asset of any biographer is his/her personal knowledge of the subject – as Anthony Alpers says with reference to Robert Browning's famous line, "the author once saw Shelley plain, and there is no substitute for that" (12)? Whether this unique situation is an advantage or a disadvantage in disguise has been a topic for debate. There are cases where the personal relation between the biographer and the subject produces disaster. The biographers in such cases are mostly relatives or close friends who may be just too close to write a reliable narrative. The commemorative instinct reigns above all other likely and often imperative considerations such as adherence to facts or objectivity. The outcome is a panegyric full of tiresome praise, distortions of fact and covering of faults.

Despite the possible abuses of the "distanceless" biographer-subject relationship, some of the genre's most famous examples are included in this category. The biographers in these works manage somehow to curb, transform, or masterfully disguise their basic commemorative instinct. This might be the most complicated author-subject relationship in literature since the intention of writing the biography of someone one knows is never pure, unambiguous or wholly altruistic. The debate of objectivity is hardly won by the biographer. In the midst of such emotional entanglement choices are not easily made when time comes to express faults or weaknesses without offering justifications. These complications aside, personal knowledge is invaluable to the creation of the sense of immediacy and lived life. Managing to recreate this immediacy on paper is the touchstone of any successful biography. These biographers are lucky: What is there to make the retelling of a life more vivid than knowing the subject's favourite walk, favourite food, the absolutely favourite poem, the tone of his/her voice when s/he speaks or the look on his/her face when s/he gets angry? Naturally each biographer uses this advantage in his/her own way, in certain cases the intimacy itself is reason enough to write a biography.

Within this category it will be interesting to look at two well-known examples of the genre: Samuel Johnson's *Life of Richard Savage* and James Boswell's *Life of Johnson*. Both biographers personally knew their subjects in varying degrees and both used this intimate knowledge to find their own way of creating a vivid portrait on paper. As Homburger and Charmley claim in *The Troubled Face of Biography* these works "[seek] to do what only the greatest art has ever done: to convey the feel of an individual's experience, to see the world as a single person saw it" (xi), their advantage being the opportunity to stand together with their subjects, at least for a certain amount of time, and look at the same world with them. Let us start with one of the most seemingly odd biographical pairs.

In 1777, a group of London based booksellers came together to publish a collection of works by English poets. They were a competitive group since a similar task was recently completed by a group of Edinburgh booksellers. However, that particular edition was criticized for its small print and errors. These London booksellers were determined to make a better effort. They would attach the name of one of the most illustrious literary figures of the land to the production of their series which would ensure profitable sales. With this in mind, they approached the then sixty-eight year old Dr Samuel Johnson (1709-1784). He was to write a biographical preface for each of the poets featured. Johnson agreed. He was no stranger to biography by then. He was both a practitioner with a series of lives written for the

Gentleman's Magazine and a theoretician with two major essays on biography in *The Rambler* No: 60 (1750) and *The Idler* No: 84 (1760) under his belt. Johnson's prefaces were published under the title *Prefaces Biographical and Critical to the Works of the English Poets*; but they came to be known by the title *Lives of the English Poets* (1779-1781). Shakespeare, Milton, Dryden, Pope, Addison, Gray, Swift are some of the names on this list of poets. However, there is one name among them that is not very readily recognized today: Richard Savage. Why would Johnson add Savage to this list? Is this the generosity of a talented man to one who is less accomplished than himself or did he consider him equal to the others? Any answer we try to find will mislead us if we ask the question thinking Savage as an integral part of this group of literary figures, for *Life of Richard Savage* does not actually belong to the series.

To place this work in its right context we need to go back thirty-three years to 1744. We also need to leave behind the older Johnson, whose name attached to any work assures profits, and go to a young Johnson who is just starting out in London, a Johnson who is just emerging from the position of a Grub Street hack "who signed his letters in 1738 'impransus' – supperless" (Holmes 9).

Johnson was writing anonymously for the *Gentleman's Magazine*. By 1742 he had published a short series of lives of scholars, physicians, scientists, priests, and others. A year later his friend, the poet Richard Savage, died, and in 1744 Johnson wrote his biography. This work, alongside poems like "London" and "The Vanity of Human Wishes," which he signed openly, established Johnson as a figure of major literary force and fame.

Why pick Savage who was little more than a frustrated genius even for his contemporaries? For the answer we need to look in two different directions. One is personal: Savage was a friend of Johnson's youth. Together they suffered poverty. Johnson made it, but Savage never did. After a life of misfortune, misunderstanding, waste, and self-destruction Savage died in prison, penniless and virtually friendless. Johnson used biography to justify Savage's ways to the public, to clear his name for posterity. Ironically, he made his friend immortal through literature, something which Savage himself was unable to realize with his own claim to genius and his literary output.

The second direction is Johnson's moralistic approach to biography which he later formulated in the two essays he wrote for *The Rambler* and *The Idler*. In *The Rambler* No: 60 he writes:

> I have often thought that there has rarely passed a life of which a judicious and faithful narrative would not be useful. For, not only every man has, in mighty mass of the world, great numbers in the same condition with himself, to whom his mistakes and miscarriages, escapes and expedients, would be of immediate and apparent use; but there is such a uniformity in the state of man, considered apart from adventitious and separable decorations and disguises, that there is scarce any possibility of good or ill but is common to human kind. (95)

If so, what better material for a biography could there be than Savage's life? Savage claimed that he was the illegitimate son of Earl Rivers and Anne Countess of Macclesfield. His parentage was never acknowledged and he never got the inheritance which he believed was due to him. He lived a life of poverty with occasional bubbles of good fortune which burst just as soon as they materialized.

Johnson opens his rendition of this "fit for fiction" life with an echo of his moralistic approach. He makes a general statement about the human condition. This is not a conventional opening for a biography. The common practice is to introduce the subject directly, in the very first paragraph. Here, we find that the introductory paragraph does not highlight an individual but what may be considered common to humanity in general, indicating that Johnson is particularly interested in the extent to which this life will awaken empathy in others, and provide them with instruction and comfort.

In this opening section Johnson states that power or fortune does not guarantee happiness. The ordinary person who possesses much of neither, falls into the mistake of believing the opposite and thinks himself unfortunate. Life is full of examples to the contrary. Since power and fortune are "extrinsic," it is understandable that they do not bring happiness. But one expects more from "intrinsic" attributes such as "intellectual greatness." Although Savage was unable to gain either power or fortune, Johnson implies that he was a literary gem and thus blessed with "intrinsic" value; however, the biography will show that this advantage is not enough either. Hence Johnson defines *Life of Savage* as "a mournful narrative." In the beginning, the Savage Johnson sees is a gifted man who suffers in life because of misfortunes beyond his control: quite an accurate statement for the early part of Savage's life, it turns out. However, Johnson seems to have never doubted the accuracy of Savage's claim to the family name which has since been discredited by subsequent research; and actually the misfortunes of Savage's later years were mostly a result of his own behaviour. Therefore, the premise Johnson opens with is somewhat contradictory to what follows, but this ambiguity is the dynamic which makes this particular biography work.

In his biography of Samuel Johnson, Walter Jackson Bate observes that "Johnson loved biography before every other kind of writing. It gives us, he said, 'what comes near to us, what we can turn to use'" (xix). Johnson's alchemy is to turn an ordinary life story into a moral narrative useful for others. For him, this is biography's main *raison d'etre* as a genre. So, before we actually see Savage, we find Johnson's moral stamp justifying this biography, assuring the reader that it will be worth the while.

Johnson the master prose writer was aware that long moralizing would not make a good read. True to the "instruct and delight" motto, he confines the introduction to four short, compact paragraphs and starts the actual narrative of the life with a gossipy, attractive sentence, illustrating his full awareness of the entertaining, voyeuristic aspect of the genre, which he is not ashamed to use.

> In the year 1697, Anne Countess of Macclesfield, having lived for some time upon very uneasy terms with her husband, thought a public confession of adultery the most obvious and expeditious method of obtaining her liberty; and therefore declared that the child with which she was then great was begotten by the Earl Rivers (501).

Johnson came from Lichfield, the place he had left as an unsuccessful school-master, to London in 1737. He was twenty-seven years old. There he met this alleged child of Earl Rivers, the forty year old Richard Savage. By then Savage was one of the most notorious figures of the London literary scene.

They were close friends for two years, just before Savage left for Bristol in 1739 through the insistence of his friends. It was interesting that "no one, at any time, or in any place, ever left a first-hand account of seeing Johnson and Savage together. It was from the start, an invisible friendship" (Holmes 35). No matter how "invisible," the friendship left a mark on Johnson. His own biographers find it puzzling. Sir John Hawkins writes, "with one person, however, he commenced an intimacy, the motives to which, at first view, may probably seem harder to be accounted for than any one particular in his life. The person was Mr. Richard Savage" (51-52). Boswell, Johnson's best-known biographer, writes the following when the time comes to introduce Savage:

> [...] a man, of whom it is difficult to speak impartially, without wondering that he was for some time the intimate companion of Johnson; for his character was marked by profligacy, insolence, and ingratitude: yet, as he understandably had a warm and vigorous, though unregulated mind, had seen life in all its varieties, and been much in the company of the

> statesmen, and wits of his time, he could communicate to Johnson an abundant supply of such materials as his philosophical curiosity most eagerly desired and as Savage's misfortunes and misconduct had reduced him to the lowest state of wretchedness as a writer for bread, his visits to St. John's Gate naturally brought Johnson and him together. (Boswell 118)

Jealous of anything and everything that has a chance of coming closer to Johnson's heart than himself, Boswell dismisses the friendship. He turns it into a calculated act on Johnson part: Since Johnson is avidly curious about human experience, Savage must have been a good source for the future writer – why else would Johnson befriend such a creature? And, of course, Johnson must have never sought Savage's company – he must have been forced into acquaintance by being much thrown together because of their similar financial situations.

But Boswell does not leave it at that; he goes out of his way to make a lengthy note on Hawkins's sensitive and acute observation in his own biography hinting that Johnson had been charmed by Savage:

> Sir John Hawkins gives the world to understand, that Johnson, 'being an admirer of genteel manners, was captivated by the address and demeanour of Savage, who as to his exterior, was, to a remarkable degree, accomplished.' Hawkins's *Life*, p. 52. But Sir John's notions of gentility must appear somewhat ludicrous, from his stating the following circumstance as presumptive evidence that Savage was a good swordsman: 'That he understood the exercise of a gentleman's weapon, may be here inferred from the use made of it in that rash encounter which is related in his life.' The dexterity here alluded to was, that Savage, in a nocturnal fit of drunkenness, stabbed a man at a coffee-house, and killed him; for which he was tried at the old Bailey, and found guilty of murder. (Boswell 118)

Boswell is blinded by his own prejudice. Although it may have been hard to understand for Boswell, Johnson *was* captivated by the charismatic Savage. They shared a short period of their lives when Johnson was quite vulnerable. The young Johnson probably saw similarities between himself and this aging poet: He was most uncertain as to the outcome of his move to London. He knew he was talented, but his talents had not yet born fruit. His grotesque physical appearance, convulsions – remnants of a childhood illness – and episodes of deep depression greatly marginalized him as a young man. He was extremely poor and most definitely angry at his misfortunes. And, in Savage, he found someone together with whom he would be angry at the world. As would be expected from a man of Johnson's acuity, he was not unaware of Savage's faults, and being frank in youth as in old age, he did not shy away from criticism where he thought criticism was due.

Savage was most probably glad to find such a bright disciple. Accounts of him tell us that he was very fond of conversation especially where he could find partial audiences to relate his misfortunes. We know from Boswell's detailed portrayal of Johnson and Johnson's *Life of Savage* that both men hated solitude, tried to find company in any which way. For that particular time between 1737 and 1739 Johnson and Savage were a perfect match.

In *Life of Savage*, we first note Johnson's acceptance of Savage's account of his birth at face value. Savage's own personal narrative derives its pathos from his illegitimacy. He did not have any documents to support his claims. His own version and consequently Johnson's version of his birth is never proved. Lady Macclesfield *did* have two illegitimate children (a boy and a girl) by Earl Rivers, the boy is registered as born on 1697 (Tracy 11), whereas Savage said that he was born in either 1697 or 1698 (Johnson 501). The names of their godmothers and nurses were different. Lady Macclesfield declared both her children dead, they are registered as dead and they have marked graves.

Johnson never expresses the slightest doubt about Savage's birth. He does what would be unpardonable in a modern biographer – he does not check his facts. But none of Savage's contemporaries seem to have doubted him. He stuck to his story so adamantly, and Lady Macclesfield kept so silent that even when Savage was brought before the court for murder and declared himself as "Richard Savage, the son of Earl Rivers" nobody thought twice about it.

A subject closely related to Savage's birth is the mother image created by Johnson in the text. Johnson greatly emphasizes the mother's "unnatural" neglect of Savage. He is forceful in passing judgement on her divorce from the Earl of Macclesfield, saying that she was paid back her fortune "undeservedly" after the divorce. Johnson anticipates the questions that would come to the reader's mind. Why would a mother do that? Johnson tries to guess the reason for such "unnatural" behaviour and finds none. He mentions certain circumstances where a mother's neglect of her child is in a way understandable such as "the dread of shame or poverty." The language Johnson uses in the long paragraph on Lady Macclesfield is quite fiery, phrases like "delight to see him struggle with misery," or "take every opportunity of aggravating his misfortunes," enables him to paint a severe picture of the circumstances beyond Savage's control. The profanation of the Madonna and child image – a baby who cannot expect protection even from his own mother – seems to bring out a thunderous, god-like wrath from Johnson and sets the tone of his reaction to life's inexplicable cruelties. Savage's mother takes on the form of a Fury bound on the destruction of a mere human. Of course, he does not display the mother as she was by then: A Mrs. Brett, the seventy-seven year old widow of Colonel Brett (the man she married after her divorce from the Earl), a reclusive woman devoted to her legitimate daughter. Johnson firmly establishes Savage's unlucky start in life:

> Such was the beginning of the life of Richard Savage. Born with a legal claim to honour and affluence, he was in two

> months illegitimated by the parliament, and disowned by his mother, doomed to poverty and obscurity, and launched upon the ocean of life, only that he might be swallowed by its quicksands or dashed upon its rocks. (502)

Readers who are used to the less emotional, non-metaphorical prose of Johnson's later works hesitate at the sudden appearance of the rather romantic landscape of the "rocks" and "oceans" of life. Young Johnson's yet not-so-well controlled emotions show through. He is angry at Savage's mother and also at English society for neglecting young Savage, which reminds one of Hogarth's pictures where children are tossed in the air like insignificant, disposable things.

Savage's mother declares to Earl Rivers at his death bed that their son is dead and the Earl believes her; but, Johnson needs to emphasize why he believes her. This he does by putting himself in the Earl's shoes and uses the episode as another opportunity to reinforce the wickedness of the mother: "the Earl did not imagine there could exist in a human form a mother that would ruin her son without enriching herself, and therefore bestowed upon some other person six thousand pounds, which he had in his will bequeathed to Savage" (504). The mother's cruelty is further emphasized when she tries to send her son to the American plantations. This time she is prevented by unknown reasons. Johnson guesses:

> perhaps she could not easily find accomplices wicked enough to concur in so cruel an action; for it may be conceived, that those who had by a long gradation of guilt hardened by their hearts against the sense of common wickedness, would yet be shocked at the design of a mother to expose her son to slavery and want, to expose him without interest, and without provocation; and Savage might on this occasion find protectors and advocates among those who had long traded in crimes, and whom compassion had never touched before. (504)

The mother, crueler than Snow-White's step-mother, manages even to shock hardened criminals. What motivates the biographer to paint such a monstrous portrait of Savage's mother? Is young Johnson here taking revenge on the women towards whom he feels strong sexual attraction, yet cannot approach easily because of his physical appearance and poverty? We know that at this particular time he was actually having problems with his wife, who was many years his senior, which constituted another source of frustration for Johnson (Holmes 25).

The misfortunes of Savage's childhood, such as the inheritance he could not get or his less-than-perfect education were further results of his start in life without proper guardianship. Along this line, his school life is of course a point where Johnson the narrator-biographer can showcase Savage's "intrinsic" asset, his burgeoning talent for literature. However Johnson has no tangible material on that part of Savage's life.[1] At this point Johnson's linguistic genius presents itself. He writes: "Here [at a small grammar school at St. Alban's] he has initiated in literature, and passed through several of the classes, with what rapidity or what applause cannot now be known" (503). The sentence actually does not say anything about Savage's success at school; however, the words "rapidity" and "applause" are picked and put into the structure of the sentence in such a way that their sounds are left in the ear of the reader and resonate with their positive connotations in the mind, creating an impression of early artistic promise, and even success in Savage's life.

What Johnson wants to achieve depends on a delicate balance. The reader should believe Savage to be genuinely talented, charming and

---

[1] In his *Dr. Johnson and Mr. Savage* (1994), Richard Holmes reminds us of a fact many scholars (except Boswell) have overlooked. For Savage's life until the time of his trial for murder in 1727, Johnson used a booklet titled *The Life of Mr. Richard Savage...Who was condemned...the last Sessions at the Old Baily, For Murder...with some very remarkable Circumstances relating to the Birth and the Education, of that Gentleman, which were never before made publick.* Holmes tells us that "Johnson followed its story line paragraph by paragraph, adding his own commentary and occasional new facts or corrections" (56).

lovable; otherwise, his failings will not create the pathos Johnson requires of the cathartic power of biography. This is a difficult task since Savage is not a universally acknowledged genius. Here is an example of how Johnson goes about recreating a talented Savage for the reader:

> It is very reasonable *to conjecture*, that this application was equal to his abilities, because his improvement was more than proportioned to the opportunities which he enjoyed; *nor can it be doubted*, that if his early productions had been preserved, like those of happier students, *might* in some have found vigorous sallies of that sprightly humour which distinguishes "The Author to be Let", and in others strong touches of that ardent imagination which painted the solemn scenes of "The Wanderer". (503; emphases mine)

On another occasion Johnson writes:

> This interval of prosperity furnished him with opportunities of enlarging his knowledge of human nature, by contemplating life from its highest gradations to its lowest; and, *had he afterwards applied* to dramatic poetry, *he would perhaps not have had* many superiors [...]. (525; emphases mine)

Johnson draws Savage's literary merits not from actually existing literary works but from the potential that he believed Savage had. This is a testament to Savage's intellectual and social deportment. Even though he was never able to fully realize his potential as far as the people around him were concerned, for such an intelligent and observant man as Johnson, that potential was never in question.

It is not uncommon in Johnson's text to come across an occasional "I do not know." Such an admission would not be quite as easy for a modern biographer, who would rather show the reader that not a single stone is left unturned while tracing the details of a life. Johnson expresses his highlights in broad strokes, therefore a few unimportant details can safely be left out. This gives the text a conversational quality. "I don't know" belongs to an age where it can honestly be uttered without damage to one's credibility.

Johnson is not very particular about his sources and uses phrases like "It is generally reported" (505) quite easily. This casual air should not be attributed to carelessness, but to Johnson's belief about biographical detail: "The incidents which give excellence to biography are of a volatile and evanescent kind, such as soon escape the memory, and are rarely transmitted by tradition" (97). This view of the nature of memory contributes to the ease of Johnson's style. However, the work is not loose in form; on the contrary, it is meticulously structured and utterly economical in expression.

There is a popular belief that Johnson wrote the work extremely fast. This belief arises from a statement attributed to Johnson in Boswell's *Journal of the Tour to the Hebrides*, "I wrote forty-eight of the printed octavo pages of the *Life of Savage* at a sitting; but then I sat up all night" (35). It has since then taken its place within the myth-making mechanism of biography. However, a recent biographer corrects us:

> It is clear from the typographical evidence of the book's printing that the epic all-night sitting refers to a single period of *rewriting*, later in January 1744. Working against a printer's deadline, Johnson recast the final section with new materials about Savage's death, and the last forty-eight pages were reset. (Holmes 55)

Young Savage discovers his real parents while going through his nurse's boxes after her death. This is a scene that would ordinarily lend itself to high dramatization. However, Johnson's presentation of it is very matter-of-fact. The young man opens to the boxes and finds "the papers" – which are incidentally never seen by anyone accept Savage's "manager," Aaron Hill, who did not make any part of it public. Johnson chooses to use his descriptive powers in another area though. The now-exposed mother's cruelty is juxtaposed with her son's longing to get acquainted with her:

> Savage was at the time so touched with the discovery of his real mother, that it was his frequent practice to walk in the dark evenings for several hours before her door, in hopes of seeing her as she might come by accident to the window, or cross her apartment with a candle in her hand. (505)

A picture of the wronged, unloved, rejected Savage standing outside his mother's window trying to catch a glimpse of his heartless mother – Johnson must have felt deeply for Savage. He writes as if he himself is wronged. This particular scene must have been a part of Savage's personal myth. There is one more scene which Johnson narrates anachronistically within the regular chronological telling of Savage's life. This second anecdote should follow closely after the quotation above but Johnson keeps it till later and by doing so strengthens its impact. He carries the anecdote to a time after Savage's conviction of murder and application for pardon from the Queen. His cruel mother tries to influence the Queen against her son, and in order to prove his violent nature, lets her know that Savage, finding the door of her house accidentally open in one of those evenings when he is taking a walk, walks in, goes upstairs without being observed by any of the servants and enters his mother's bedroom. She is shocked, cries out, accuses him of trying to kill her and gets him thrown out.

As explained by Johnson, Savage's behaviour may seem like an impulsive, passionate gesture, a final reaching out brutally suppressed. The following sentence at the end of the anecdote is successful in creating that impression: "Savage who had attempted with the most submissive tenderness to soften her rage, hearing her utter so detestable an accusation, thought it prudent to retire; and, I believe, never attempted afterwards to speak to her" (520). Later biographies, especially modern ones like Tracy's and Holmes's urge us to consider the anecdote from the mother's point of view. Savage's behaviour may indeed be as Holmes says that of "'an incessant' and perhaps obsessive prowler" (75).

We have so far seen Savage standing in front of his mother's house at night, entering that house another night. Perhaps the most prominent image of the miniature legend of Savage and Johnson's friendship also involves the night. This image owes its popularity not to Johnson's *Life of Savage* but rather to the accounts of Hawkins and Boswell in their biographies of Johnson. First Boswell's version:

> It is melancholy to reflect, that Johnson and Savage were sometimes in such extreme indigence, that they could not pay for a lodging; so that they have wandered together whole nights in the streets. Yet in those incredible scenes of distress, we may suppose that Savage mentioned many of the anecdotes with which Johnson afterwards enriched the life of his unhappy companion, and those of other Poets. (Boswell 119)

Now Hawkins's account:

> Johnson has told me, that whole nights have been spent by him and Savage in conversations of this kind, not under the hospitable roof of a tavern, where warmth might have invigorated their spirits, and wine dispelled their care; but in a perambulation round the squares of Westminster, St James's in particular, when all the money they could raise was less than sufficient to purchase for them the shelter and sordid comforts of a night cellar. Of the result of their conversation little can now be known, save, that they gave rise to those principles of patriotism, that both, for some years after, avowed. (53-54)

But note how Johnson writes the same scene, carefully extracting himself from the picture:

> [Savage] lodged as much by accident as he dined, and passed the night sometimes in mean houses, which are set open at night to any casual wanderers, sometimes in cellars, among the riot and filth of the meanest and most profligate; and sometimes, when he had not money to support even the expenses of these receptacles, walked about the streets till he was weary, and lay down in the summer upon a bulk, or in winter with his associates in poverty, among the ashes of a glass-house.
>
> In this manner were passed those days and those nights which nature had enabled him to have employed in elevated speculations, useful studies, or pleasing conversation. On a bulk, in a cellar, or in glass-house among thieves and beggars, was to be found the Author of *The Wanderer*, the man of exalted sentiments, extensive views, and curious observations; the man whose remarks on life might have assisted the statesman, whose ideas of virtue might have enlightened the moralist, whose eloquence might have influenced senates, and whose delicacy might have polished courts. (556-57)

The admiration, pity, human compassion, and frustration felt at fate and society that is evident in these two paragraphs sum up the whole tone of *Life of Savage*. A careful look will show that Johnson did away with the "together." In his version Savage is alone except a passing mention of "his associates in poverty." This lonely figure casts two shadows. First, it creates the Savage Johnson wanted the readers to know, so well expressed by Holmes:

> So when Johnson came to write Savage's *Life* in 1743, he put Savage's night-walking at the heart of the story of his literary career. He did it so powerfully that he created a legend, almost an eighteenth-century archetype, of the Outcast Poet

> moving through an infernal cityscape, the 'City of Dreadful Night', in which his eye alone witnesses the horror, filth and misery that the rich and powerful have created as they slumber, uncaring. (45)

Secondly, he detaches himself from Savage. He had chosen a different path and he had used his energy not as a force for self-destruction like his friend but as a force of self-creation, one outcome of which was writing Savage's life – as if he were looking at himself from behind the shadows and deciding to be otherwise.

Johnson particularly wants to illustrate Savage's incessant drive to create and he is quite successful with the following scene:

> During a considerable part of the time in which he was employed upon this performance, he was without lodging, and often without meat; nor had he any other conveniences for study than the fields or the street allowed to him; there he used to walk and form his speeches, and afterwards step into a shop, beg for a few moments the use of the pen and ink, and write down what he had composed, upon paper which he had picked up by accident. (512)

After having seen the conditions under which Savage wrote, we may now look at how Johnson approaches Savage's literary works. His attitude to writing is not presented as that of a person who sees literary work as a vocation. Half tongue in cheek and half seriously Johnson writes how Savage came to write after he lost hope of any financial gain from his mother: "He was therefore obligated to seek other means of support; and, having no profession became by necessity an author" (506). Savage's writing habits support the serious vein in this statement. He tried his hand in any kind of writing which he believed to be profitable at the time, including the theatre. "But having been unsuccessful in comedy, though rather for want of opportunities than genius, he resolved now to try whether he should not be more fortunate in exhibiting a tragedy" (512).

Johnson notes Savage's practical approach to writing to show how financial worries affect literary production. He is sure of Savage's genius. This certainty and Savage's several failures are reconciled in the central idea that external circumstances more often than not shape, confine, and possibly blunt genius. They prevent it from being fully realized. Such a waste is greatly to be pitied. "If the performance of a writer thus distressed is not perfect, its faults ought surely to be imputed to a cause very different from want of genius, and must rather excite pity than provoke censure" (513).

Having established this point, Johnson takes extreme care to evaluate each work fairly. We must keep in mind that *Life of Savage* is not a critical "life and works" type of biography. Therefore, Johnson avoids long, detailed analyses but nonetheless makes comments. His tone is not different in these sections; he does not assume a strictly critical, professional tone. There are works that he likes and elegantly praises such as the poems "The Author to be Let," "The Wanderer" and "The Bastard." And there are others he is not very pleased with, such as Savage's dedication to *A Miscellany of Poems:*

> The Dedication is addressed to Lady Mary Wortley Montagu whom he flatters without reserve, and to confess the truth, with very little art. The same observation may be extended to all his Dedications: his compliments are constrained and violent, heaped together without the grace of order, or the decency of introduction; he seems to have written his panegyrics for the perusal only of his patrons, and to have imagined that he had no other task than to pamper them with praises however gross, and that flattery would make its way into the heart, without the assistance of elegance or invention. (515)

Whatever the evaluation, Johnson dwells insistently on the fact that Savage wrote all his work under dire circumstances. The attitudes of the supposed "patrons" of the arts – members of the government, nobility and even royalty to whom Savage often dedicates his works in hopes of a cash reward, helps Johnson illustrate the point that society is indifferent and often cruel to its promising individuals. The artistic temperament is left to survive without support or encouragement.

Johnson employs the same device of subtle manipulation he uses while writing about Savage's intellectually promising childhood, in commenting on Savage's work. A poem called "The Progress of a Freethinker," which Savage only plans but never writes, gets the following comment from him:

> That he did not execute this design is a real loss to mankind, for he was too well acquainted with all the scenes of debauchery to have failed in his representation of them, and too zealous for virtue not to have represented them in such a manner as should expose them either to ridicule or detestation. (550)

Johnson also explores Savage's lack of conviction in writing. Savage does not have much difficulty in praising someone whom he actually detests. For example, he praises Sir Robert Walpole in writing while in real life he frequently condemns him and his politics. At this point Johnson anticipates the reader's question: "Why?" The answer, a defence in disguise, is very human: Savage writes to please the man who feeds and clothes him at the time. Johnson is careful in pointing out that Savage was aware of what he was doing, lamenting "the misery of living at the tables of other men."

The discussion of his works presents the reader with a vivid image of Savage's practices. These small intimate details are the ones that create the sense of immediacy in the biography; they add the sense of lived, everyday life. The advantage of the biographer who knows his subject is obvious here. Johnson mentions his friend's diligence in proof reading and correction, and how meticulous he was especially in correcting punctuation, a somewhat unexpected detail about a man who gives the impression of being utterly careless.

Johnson does not use the advantage of personal knowledge explicitly, although this intimate knowledge forms the backbone of biographical writing as he himself claims in an essay: "[...] more knowledge may be gained of man's real character, by a short conversation with one of his servants, than from formal and studied narrative, begun with his pedigree, and ended in his funeral" (*The Rambler* 97). In fact, he uses this idea to inform the whole texture of the narrative, giving the illusion that the text, like life itself, is just "there," existing in its own right without the constant presence/interruption of an observer/narrator.

Johnson's personal view of issues can sometimes be sensed from his particular emphasis on certain works. For example he discusses "On Public Spirit, with Regards to Public Works" quite extensively since this poem concerns itself with issues which Johnson himself is interested in such as the immigration to America and the interaction between the new settlers and the natives.

When he detects self-deception on Savage's part, Johnson does not blindly take his side: A poem Savage writes for the Prince goes unnoticed and its general reception is very poor. Only seventy two copies are sold. This time Johnson stands aside and lets the reader see the nature of Savage's self-deception:

> But Savage easily reconciled himself to mankind without imputing any defect to his work, by observing that his poem was unluckily published two days after the prorogation of the parliament, and by consequence at a time when all those who could be expected to regard it were in the hurry of preparing for their departure, or engaged in taking leave of others upon their discussion from public affairs. (555)

Johnson takes the side of the public saying that the poem did not actually deserve attention.

If Savage does not have an inheritance and if he cannot make a decent, steady living by his pen, how could he survive? Through friends. One of the strengths of *Life of Savage* is Johnson's ability to give life to peripheral characters around Savage. A benefit of Savage's literary endeavours is that they get him introduced to men and women who are able to help him in some way. How these friends enter Savage's life is told through anecdotes, the sources of which Johnson never discloses; even when the source is himself, he does not declare it openly. He seems to go to great lengths to withdraw from the story as a participant and chooses to act only as the narrative voice.

Like a protective parent Johnson sometimes approves and sometimes disapproves of Savage's friends. Of his extravagant friend Sir Richard Steele, the well-known essayist and dramatist, Johnson tells an anecdote and then proceeds to write:

> Under such a tutor, Mr. Savage was not likely to learn prudence or frugality; and perhaps many of the misfortunes, which the want of those virtues brought upon him in the following part of his life, might be justly imputed to so unimproving an example. (508)

There are others like the actor Robert Wilks and the actress Anne Oldfield. The latter is so charmed by Savage, enjoys his conversation so much, and is so moved by his misfortunes that she decides to give him fifty pounds a year as long as she lives. Here, Johnson tries to dispel any suspicion of her being Savage's mistress. He repeats Savage's words that they were never alone together and adds that Savage showed his regard for her after her death "by wearing mourning as for a mother" (510).

Johnson is of course unaware of a letter Savage wrote in 1739 in which he takes back his story of the fifty pounds and Theophilus Cibber, in his *Lives of the Poets* (1753) paints a different picture of Mrs Oldfield and Savage:

> But she so much disliked the man, and disapproved of his conduct, that she never admitted him to her conversation, nor suffered him to enter her house. She indeed, often relieved him with such donations, as spoke her generous disposition. But this was on the solicitation of friends, who frequently set his calamities before her in the most piteous light [...] (Holmes 64)

Biographer Richard Holmes adds a few more details about this quotation:

> Annotating Johnson's *Life* in 1753, Cibber added that Savage's veracity was not 'greatly to be depended on', and that in this as in other matters the 'good natured' Johnson had 'suffered his better understanding to be misled'. (64)

What was the source of this charm? A futile question. Savage obviously had that "je ne sais quoi" which did not make Johnson doubt for a single moment when Savage said a woman was charmed by him enough to give him a yearly allowance of fifty pounds (a sum which would be sufficient for a whole family to be "above want" for a year).

Johnson does not talk about the first time they met, the initial impression Savage made on him or his later influence. He does not even describe what Savage looks like until the very end. Nevertheless, we can deduce the elements of Savage's charm from the text. The following must give some indication of Johnson's own feelings:

> To admire Mr. Savage was a proof of discernment; and to be acquainted with him, was a title to poetical reputation. His presence was sufficient to make any place of public entertainment popular; and his approbation and example constituted the fashion. (525)

Savage certainly had presence. The Scottish poet James Thomson met him when he came to London, like Johnson, in search of a better fortune. Since we do not have Johnson's account, let us hear Thomson's first impressions of Savage:

> The scribbling rhyming generation (lord deliver us!) buzz and swarm here like insects on a summer's day, and are as noxious: so that every coffee-house shop and stall in town crawl with their maggots. One vengeful hornet (Savage, if you'll indulge me a pun at his name) so plagued and stung me yesterday, with everlasting repetition, as provokes me to this rude-perhaps-complaint [...] for my part I renounce the tuneful starving trade. (Sambrook 25)

Despite these unfavourable first impressions, the charm worked and Thomson became one of Savage's most faithful and indulgent friends. Savage was also successful in securing the friendship of Alexander Pope, whom he was "suspected of supplying with private intelligence and secret incidents" (Johnson, *Life of Savage* 528) for the *Dunciad.* Johnson states that Pope's friendship was very important for Savage, especially since Pope turned out to be one of his most reliable friends until the end of Savage's life.

Fortunate as he was to be surrounded by many who were ready to help him, Savage was not very grateful for his good fortune, nor was he careful of it. His friendship with his benefactors ended bitterly. He ridiculed Sir Richard Steele, and Sir Richard in turn stopped his allowance, and never again let him into his house. The incident is presented from both sides, and there is an omniscient interjection by the God-like voice of Johnson who says:

> A little knowledge of the world is sufficient to discover that such weakness is very common, and that there are few who do not sometimes, in the wantonness of thoughtless mirth, or the heat of transient resentment speak of their friends and benefactors with levity and contempt, though in their cooler moments they want neither sense of their kindness, nor rever-

> ence for their virtue. The fault therefore of Mr. Savage was rather negligence than ingratitude; but Sir Richard must likewise be acquitted of severity, for who is there that can patiently bear contempt from one whom he has relieved and supported, whose establishment he has laboured, and whose interest he has promoted? (509)

He also shows such "negligence" towards Lord Tyrconnel, his mother's legitimate son who took him into his family, agreed to give him two hundred pounds a year "upon his promise to lay aside his design of exposing the cruelty of his mother" (525). But his unruly behaviour causes a quarrel during which Savage accuses Tyrconnel of not being generous enough. With this quarrel, what Johnson calls "Savage's golden times" come to an end. Johnson uses this instance to show that the popularity Savage enjoyed during that time was to a large extent "the lustre of the ornaments of wealth added to genius" (525). Both parties refuse to reconcile; and again Johnson draws the reader's attention to how people who can not stand much injury through quarrels also bear grudges, how their pride can get easily hurt. Savage himself did not like to be ridiculed, but strangely enough, he did not find this a reason not to ridicule others.

This is a good place to look at Johnson's psychological insight into Savage's behaviour. Johnson sees Savage's ingratitude as an opportunity to understand an aspect of human psychology: "It is too common for those who have unjustly suffered pain, to inflict it likewise in their turn with the same injustice, and to imagine that they have a right to treat others as they have themselves been treated" (537). Although Savage fails to observe many of the unwritten rules of friendship, he gets away with it most of the time. He is able to make new friends to take the place of the ones he lost:

> This conduct indeed very seldom drew upon him those inconveniences that might be feared by any other person; for his conversation was so entertaining, and his address so

> pleasing, that few thought the pleasure which they received from him dearly purchased, by paying him for his wine. It was his particular happiness, that he scarcely ever found a stranger, whom he did not leave a friend, but it must likewise be added, that he had not often a friend long, without obliging him to become a stranger. (533)

Through his relationship with friends, one sees how impulsive Savage is. He is guided by his emotions and he does not really calculate the outcome of quarrels especially with the influential and powerful. His artless, impulsive side gives us a hint of what might constitute his charm for Johnson. In such cases, he must have been genuine, someone who can be described by "what you see is what you get." Johnson notices Savage's tendency to blame others for his sufferings. He takes such a projection and turns it into a universal trait: "By arts like these, arts which everyman practices in some degree, and which too much of the tranquillity of life is to be ascribed, Savage was always able to live at peace with himself" (541-42). He grasps Savage's weakness:

> [...] it is certain that he was upon every occasion too easily reconciled to himself, and that he appeared very little to regret those practices which had impaired his reputation. The reigning error of his life was, that he mistook the love for the practice of virtue, and was indeed not so much a good man, as the friend of goodness. (542-43)

A crucial event of Savage's life is his killing James Sinclair in a brawl in a coffee-house. Johnson relates the incident of 20 November 1727 in a matter-of-fact manner. The passage is written in the passive voice which helps dissociate Savage from the act of murder: "swords were drawn on both sides and one Mr. James Sinclair was killed" (516). Johnson refuses to speculate on the action and passes directly on to the trial. He emphasizes that the trial depended on the credibility of the testimonies. The witnesses against Savage are discredited because of their low social status, and the readers, like the court, are reminded of Savage's clean past.

Savage defends himself in an hour-long speech which Johnson does not quote directly but paraphrases, moving on to the effect it had "on the multitude that thronged the court" (518). Johnson accuses the judge on the bench of "insolence and severity" and his speech is parodied. We learn from Johnson that Savage used to parody this man. The text echoes Savage's words and mocks him in a way which brings his competence into question. The judge is represented as a harsh man and Johnson insinuates that, given these circumstances and such ridiculous and incompetent people, poor Savage was of course convicted of murder. To aid his subtle defence of Savage in the murder case, Johnson at this moment inserts Lady Macclesfield's ultimate unfathomable malevolence towards her son into the story. Lady Macclesfield lets the Queen know about Savage's break into her house, hoping to block his pardon. However, the intervention is unsuccessful; Savage is pardoned. At this point Johnson again dives into the reasons behind a mother's cruelty. This obviously works as a distraction from the murder for which Savage seems to show no apparent remorse except that "he was unwilling to dwell upon it" (523).

Just as Johnson's partisanship reaches its zenith in his defence of Savage in the murder case, so does his attack on Savage's mother. Johnson's attitude shows us that when a biographer is writing the life of a contemporary, the biography may be used as a platform on which to exhibit the parties that affected the subject in the most negative way. In this particular case, Johnson's tone becomes accusatory and severely judgemental against Savage's mother. What the subject himself could not do during his life time is realized by the biographer, and he is vindicated by the written word which will no doubt outlive – especially since it is written by Johnson – any verbal accusation that may have been made at the time.

Johnson's accusation of Savage's mother creates an expectancy in the reader for retribution. The narrative makes the case so effectively that the reader learns to dislike so unfeeling a mother and desires some form of recompense in Savage's name. Johnson, pacing the narrative competently, provides this scene after the publication of Savage's poem *The Bastard*, where Savage "recounts the real calamities which he suffered by the crime of his parents" (540). It provides a sense of closure: a cruel mother put to right at last. It is interesting to note that the weapon of revenge is a poem. The written word, its repetition and transmission by word of mouth finally punish the mother. Johnson's prose reflects the delicious feeling of justice:

> [T]he wretch who had, without scruple, proclaimed herself an adulteress, and who had first endeavoured to starve her son, then to transport him, and afterwards to hang him, was not able to bear the representation of her conduct; but fled from reproach, though she felt no pain from guilt, and left Bath with the utmost haste, to shelter herself among the crowds of London.
>
> Thus Savage had the satisfaction of finding, that; though he could not reform his mother, he could punish her, and that he did not always suffer alone. (540-41)

The mother's conduct finally finds its place within the moral fibre of the story. Her behaviour at the time of her son's appeal for pardon is compared to the conduct of the countess of Hertford who intervened on Savage's behalf and finally persuaded the Queen: "no one can fail to observe how much more amiable it is to relieve, than to oppress, and to rescue innocence from destruction, than to destroy without an injury" (522). Note that the word "innocence" is used in conjunction with a man who admitted to murder, and did not show any apparent sign of remorse.

Johnson does the same to a lesser degree in one other instance: the small revenge taken on James Miller. Miller once ridiculed Savage's acting in a farce at the theatre, "insinuating that Savage had but one coat" (559). Savage got extremely angry and wrote a lampoon against him; however, he later decided not to publish it. Johnson praises Savage's decision of withdrawing the attack; but, he also does something else, he makes the injury public, exposing Miller's cruelty and exalting Savage's forgiving nature simultaneously.

Here, we start to realize that Johnson separates the actions from the man. He believes in Savage's innate innocence which in his eyes remain untainted by any foul action. Along this line, conviction for murder is Johnson's biggest challenge. For the man to receive compassion and even pity, for him to constitute an example, Johnson is anxious to re-establish Savage's decent character – a character whom the reader should find ultimately lovable, forgivable, and believable. Johnson draws our attention to the two key witnesses in Savage's trial: a woman who later retracted her testimony and a man who was strongly suspected to be drunk at the time of the murder. Attacking the credibility of the witnesses and the evidence, Johnson tries to bring the damaging effect of the murder trial on Savage's life to a minimum. "When all these particulars are rated together, perhaps the memory of Savage may not be much sullied by his trial" (522). To clean up his image further, Johnson tells a moving anecdote the truth of which is not supported by any acknowledged source:

> Some time after he had obtained his liberty, he met in the street the woman that had sworn with so much malignity against him. She informed him, that she was in distress, and, with a degree of confidence not easily attainable, desired him to relieve her. He, instead of insulting her misery, and taking pleasure in the calamities of one who had brought his life into danger, reproved her gently for her perjury; and changing the only guinea that he had, divided it between her and himself. (522)

Johnson calls the act as one that

> in some ages would have made a saint, and perhaps in other a hero, and which, without any hyperbolical encomiums, must be allowed to be an instance of uncommon generosity, an act of complicated virtue; by which he at once relieved the poor, corrected the vicious, and forgave an enemy. (523)

The fact that Savage is not bitter is important for the moral edge of Johnson's reconstruction. However, Johnson must have realized that by whitewashing Savage he may have hurt his credibility as a biographer who wants to present life as it is. Therefore, this praise is balanced by a paragraph of almost equal length (and which immediately follows this) where Johnson notes the fact that Savage sometimes could bear grudges. Johnson does not forget to inquire into Savage's self-perception after the murder. Here, we see Savage as a character who does not want to dwell on the subject too much but who does not wholly absolve himself from guilt.

The notoriety caused by the trial brings Savage a twisted sort of fame. He continues to live day to day, hand to mouth, immediately spending what he earns or borrows. He wants to become the Poet Laureate and "prosecute[s] his application with so much diligence" (543) that the King says he will consider him for the position. But once again Savage's hopes are dashed when Colley Cibber is given the position. Bitterly disappointed, Savage does "something unique in the annals of official patronage" (Holmes 143). He declares himself Queen Caroline's "Volunteer Laureate" and announces that he will write a birthday poem for her annually. Here, Johnson inserts a letter Savage prefaced to the first such poem when it was reprinted in the *Gentleman's Magazine*. It is an odd piece, explaining in the third person the circumstances in which the poem was written. Savage wants to make sure that he gets royal recognition this time. He seems to find a way to ensure this favour by making it public so neither of the parties can step back from their obligation without public embarrassment.

Johnson, however, does not regard the Queen's acceptance and purchase of the poem favourably:

> [...] to chain down the genius of a writer to an annual panegyric, shewed in the Queen too much desire of hearing her own praises, and greater regard to herself than to him on whom her bounty was conferred. It was a kind of avaricious generosity, by which flattery was rather purchased, than genius rewarded. (545)

Actually the Queen does not pay anything but fifty pounds for the poems he writes. To this is added the accusations of influencing the vote against the Queen "by appearing at the head of a Tory mob," and later, the publication of an obscene pamphlet, both of which turn out to be groundless as far as Johnson is concerned. What Johnson does not know is that the Scotland Yard is seriously suspicious of Savage and accumulates a report on his political activities and h1e is also a writer of erotic songs (Holmes 69). The latter accusation greatly hurts Savage's reputation but Johnson says that "it is proper to secure his memory from reproach" and that Savage did not mean any harm by it.

In the meantime, Savage disappears from sight, as he was known to do whenever he had cash at his disposal; spends all the money given by the Queen, and re-emerges penniless. The thoughtless spending is presented as yet another lesson to be drawn from this destitute life. As the years go by, the help his friends provide for him becomes an obligation rather than a favour in Savage's eyes. He dares to get seriously annoyed when people refuse to help or give any hint that they expect to be paid back. Johnson openly puts this before the reader without comment, but he comments on Savage's pride even during his most difficult times. He tells an anecdote where Savage refuses the anonymous donation of a new pair of shoes and a suit left for him at a coffee-house he frequents. He makes new acquaintances "whose kindness had not been exhausted," and finds short term solutions to his immediate needs. Savage's strange pride which acts up at the most unexpected instances must have intrigued Johnson, who admiringly writes: “He never admitted any gross familiarities, or submitted to be treated otherwise than as an equal” (558).

Johnson’s Savage emerges through the progression of the text as an extremely naïve character – almost as an overgrown child. He seems strongly immune to self-doubt or self-reflection, a fact which must have fascinated Johnson. He reserves the right to be loved and be looked after at all times, no matter how he behaves. With his astonishing talent for self-delusion, he manages to perceive each situation just as he likes, so that his ego is perfectly protected.

When Savage hits rock-bottom financially the narrative arrives at one of its high-points. After all that has happened to Savage, he now gets what seems to be a last and good chance for reform. An interesting proposal comes from Pope to the effect that Savage should retire to Wales with the help of his friends, live very cheaply without any debts, and write. Savage accepts the proposal and leaves London. The departure affords the only scene that explicitly takes place between Johnson and Savage in the text. “Full of salutary resolutions, he left London in July 1739, having taken leave with great tenderness of his friends, and parted from the author of this narrative with tears in his eyes” (569). “Tears in *whose* eyes?” asks the biographer Holmes, saying that the punctuation leads the reader to believe that it is Johnson who is crying.

> It is almost as if Johnson was impelled as a friend to bear witness to his own tears, but was embarrassed as a biographer to admit them in public. This embarrassment at the strength of his feelings for Savage, when he later looked back at it, provides us with a first clue to the whole story.
>
> When Johnson came to correct the second edition of the *Life* in 1748, he noted carefully in the margin next to the “tears in his eyes” an explanatory phrase: “I had then a slight fever.” This seems to imply that Johnson was indeed recalling his own tears and emo-

> tion at losing Savage, but felt awkward doing so, and subsequently wished to dismiss them as mere physical weakness, as temporary illness. (15)

This emotional ambiguity explains the narrative mood of the *Life of Savage*: It is an ebb and flow between apology and criticism, forgiveness and judgement, partiality and objectivity, compassionate memory and moral tale.

The effect of Savage's acceptance of Pope's proposal is a sign of relief for the reader. Page after page of frustration, misfortune and misconduct is left behind, finally Savage will be well, and he will be free to do what he does best: write poems. The empathy that the reader feels is the product of Johnson's presentation. Just as one feels for the protagonist of a novel, one feels for Savage, and wants one's "practical interest" (in the narrative) – to borrow a term from Wayne Booth – to be satisfied.

Savage makes his resolutions to start all over again and believes that he will succeed. This idea of a new beginning is also very poignant for the reader, yet this occasion is another example of the extent to which Savage lacks self-knowledge and a realistic awareness of his own inclinations:

> Mr Savage however was satisfied, and willing to retire, and was convinced that the allowance, though scanty, would be more than sufficient for him, being now determined to commence a rigid economist, and to live according to the exactest rules of frugality; for nothing was in his opinion more contemptible than a man, who, when he knew his income, exceeded it, and yet he confessed, that instances of such folly were too common, and lamented that some men were not to be trusted with their own money. (569)

This ironic passage has both a light and a dark side to it. On the one hand, we desperately wish Savage to succeed, on the other, we are once again reminded of his self-denial of dramatic proportions.

Savage leaves for Swansea, yet gets only as far as Bristol, with all the money already spent. He makes new acquaintances on the way and supports himself by their means for a while. When he finally gets to Swansea, he does not have enough to build the idyllic life he dreamt he would lead there. Again, he gets angry not at himself but his benefactors whom he believes have cheated him by getting rid of him for such a small sum, and by not keeping their promise of a liberal income. Johnson is again on Savage's side:

> But it must be granted, that the diminution of his allowance was a great hardship, and that those who withdrew their subscription from a man, who, upon the faith of their promise, had gone into a kind of banishment, and abandoned all those by whom he had been before relieved in his distress, will find it no easy task to vindicate their conduct. (571)

The unconventional hours he keeps, his conversation continuing well into the small hours of the morning (a trait shared with Johnson), and most importantly his unpaid debts cause his friends to withdraw one by one. He falls into extreme misery:

> His conduct had already wearied some of those who were at first enamoured of his conversation, but he might, perhaps, still have devolved to others, whom he might have entertained with equal success, had not the decay of his clothes made it no longer consistent with their vanity to admit him to their tables, or to associate with him in public places. He now began to find every man from home at whose house he called; and was therefore no longer able to procure the necessities of life, but wandered about the town, slighted and ne-

> glected, in quest of a dinner, which he did not always obtain. (573)

Finally, with a dramatic touch, he gets arrested on his birthday for his debts. Here Johnson inserts a letter Savage wrote in prison, recipient unacknowledged. We hear Savage's own voice, a different voice from the one in the previous letter he wrote for the *Gentlemen's Magazine*. The letter does not betray any depression or ill-will, he seems to be glad to have finally found a lodging. With two other letters, Johnson shows how he refuses help and cheerfully accepts his fate. This cheerfulness under such circumstances must have astounded the depressive Johnson and perhaps prompted him to censure Savage's conduct less harshly than he might otherwise have done since it showed a joy of life he himself lacked.

The jailer and the keeper of the prison treat him like a guest. He spends his time writing, receiving visitors and chatting to "criminals." In the meantime, his health declines but he cannot call a doctor, he dies on the night of 1 August 1743 and is buried at the keeper's expense.

The death scene, which is not dramatized at all but plainly narrated as are all the other crucial moments of Savage's life, is followed by the only description of Savage's physical appearance in the biography. It seems that as Savage's life and Johnson's narrative come to a conclusion, the face of the subject appears; the description is now complete. The text, which provides the light and shade of Savage's character, almost recreates the human being already dead before the text is written. Only someone who has looked another in the face can give the following description which strikes one by its simple intimacy:

> He was of middle stature, of a thin habit of the body, a long visage, coarse features, and melancholy aspect, of a grave and manly deportment, a solemn dignity of mien; but which, upon a nearer acquaintance, softened into an engaging easiness of manner. His walk was slow, and his voice tremulous

> and mournful. He was easily excited to smiles, but very seldom provoked to laughter. (582)

This causes a surprise in the reader. One does not expect the charming, energetic, aggressive Savage to be a small man with a mournful expression.

The paragraphs that follow reveal the personal acquaintance between the biographer and his subject. It is a personal look at the man's character, mind, knowledge, works, conversation, and daily conduct. Details only to be known through personal observation are sprinkled into these last four pages: "He could not easily leave off, when he had once begun to mention himself or his works; nor ever read his verses without stealing his eyes from the page, to discover, in the faces of his audience, how they were affected with any favourite passage" (584). Every brush stroke is carefully added – a three-dimensional character emerges. The sense is of personal knowledge and compassion.

True to Edgar Allan Poe's magical formula for maximum impact, *Life of Savage* can be read at one sitting. The technical skill and economy with which it is written makes it an easy, almost breathless read of three or four hours. Here is how Sir Joshua Reynolds reacted to the *Life* according to Boswell's account:

> Sir Joshua Reynolds told me, that upon his return from Italy he met with it [*Life of Savage*] in Devonshire, knowing nothing of its author, and began to read it while he was standing with his arm leaning against a chimney-piece. It seized his attention so strongly, that, not being able to lay down the book till he had finished it, when he attempted to move, he found his arm totally benumbed. (121)

Within this relatively short work – especially if we think of the traditional biography of hundreds of pages – Johnson is in constant control of his material. He chooses to be apparently invisible, occasionally using the first person pronoun in phrases like "whose name I am now unable to recollect" (511), implying the strong ties between the biographer's memory and his subject in "distanceless" life-writing. Since, for Johnson, the only kind of decent biography is written by people who have "eat and drunk and lived in social intercourse with their subjects," Johnson's references to his memory show that the record of a man's or woman's life is in the memory of the people who knew him, and that such knowledge can easily evaporate.

The voice of the one who remembers – in this case Johnson – overlooks the whole text in a god-like manner. This omniscient voice blends itself masterfully with the background. It invites the reader to take Savage as Johnson believed him to be. In the narrative voice there is an apparently perfect balance of judgement and compassion. In this sense, the biography exudes a strange feeling of comfort – a sense of Savage being defended by a sharp advocate at a final judgement. If there were indeed a final judgement, it would not be so bad to have a Johnson to speak out for us.

The biography gets its primary strength from the narrative voice's understanding of human frailty and motivation. The text gives the impression of duplicating the effect Savage must have had on his friends. The man is in front of one's eyes with all his virtues and vices; reading the story of his life, one cannot help but condemn the man, but at every turn Johnson's voice absolves him, bringing him closer to the reader who is yet another "sinner."

The text charms just like Savage must have done. Reading about the harsh justice that catches up with Savage in prison, one does not feel a sense of satisfied closure but rather a sadness and a strong sense of wasted life, misdirected energy and anger at the uncontrollable forces that inevitably direct one's life – even though one is plainly aware of Savage's faults which play a major role in his downfall. Johnson's voice always finds a way to bestow on the subject the balm of human kindness. In a sense, the text becomes the revenge that Savage was unable to take for all the suffering life had to offer him. And through *Life of Savage*, we see Johnson weave a moral, exciting and almost romantic eulogy from the mingled threads of Savage's chaotic, dissolute life and his own younger, less magisterial self.

* * *

Personal acquaintance between biographer and subject is not always expressed in such a "brief [and] ordered" (Shelston 43) manner as in *Life of Savage*. There is another way epitomized by *the* biography of all time. In this far reach of the pendulum's swing we find Johnson again; but this time as the subject of the most famous biography in the English language: James Boswell's *The Life of Samuel Johnson, LL.D*.

"So we drove on that stage in the dark, and were long pensive and silent" (Boswell 705). Few biographies can boast of a sentence such as this. The "we" are Samuel Johnson and his friend and biographer James Boswell. Boswell's biography abounds in sentences like the one above, for as a biographer he chose to be fully present in his narrative both as a guiding, interpreting narrator, and also as a character. Boswell personally knew Johnson in the last twenty-one years of Johnson's life. Only 276 days of these were spent in Johnson's company (Nicolson 102). This creates an imbalance in the text: The major part of Johnson's life (approximately two-thirds) before Johnson met Boswell is covered in the first 250 of the colossal volume of 1400 pages, while the last third of his life is the subject of the remaining 1150. However, this gross disproportion is well concealed. The biography is organized by year, which greatly contributes to the impression of uniformity. Although the first part depends entirely on indirect accounts of the subject, the inclusion of letters and anecdotes provide a smooth and barely noticeable transition into the accounts of the later years where the primary material is Boswell's own direct observations, notes, letters, and recorded conversations.

James Boswell was born in 1740. He studied law at Edinburgh and Glasgow. He spent his professional life practicing law at the Edinburgh bar; but frequently visited London. He met Johnson in 1763, and became his friend and correspondent. He published two quite successful books, *Account of Corsica* (1768) and *Journal of the Tour to the Hebrides* (1785). After Johnson's death, he sat down to put together the material he collected on Johnson with the specific intention of writing his biography.

Since his subject was one of the most important literary figures of the time, and at least eleven other biographies were published during the seven years between Johnson's death and the publication of Boswell's biography in 1791 (Parke 41), he was anxious to establish his legitimacy. After all, the friendship of a mere Mr. Boswell may not have been creditable enough. This process of legitimization starts outside the main text, in the dedication and the advertisements to the first and second editions. Boswell dedicates his work to the famous painter, art critic and founding member of *The Literary Club*, Sir Joshua Reynolds. The overall implication of this dedication is that Boswell is capable of recognizing and appreciating greatness when he sees it: certainly an indispensable skill for a biographer. A second, and maybe equally important, implication is that the great men of his acquaintance like him well enough to reciprocate. Boswell is anxious to prove that his friendship with Johnson is not a mere coincidence and an oddity, and that other men of almost Johnson's calibre also approve of him and even befriend him.

> If a man may indulge an honest pride, in having it known to the world, that he has been thought worthy of particular attention by a person of the first eminence in the age in which he lived, whose company has been courted, I am justified in availing myself of the usual privilege of a Dedication, when I mention that there has been a long and uninterrupted friendship between us. (1)

Picking a member of *The Club* for his dedication is also a signal reminding the reader that this Scottish lawyer is one of "them": part of a distinguished, intellectual London group whose members include writer Goldsmith, philosopher Burke, actor Garrick, economist Adam Smith, and Shakespeare editor Malone alongside Reynolds and Johnson. Being the particular friend of one of these men is a strong recommendation and the stamp of approval Boswell needs.

He also establishes the fact that he has already written about Johnson and is as capable of understanding him as Reynolds does:

> You, my dear Sir, studied him, and knew him well: you venerated and admired him. Yet, luminous as he was upon the whole, you perceive all the shades, which mingled in the grand composition, all the little peculiarities and slight blemishes which marked the literary Colossus. Your very warm commendation of the specimen which I gave in my *Journal of a Tour to the Hebrides*, of my being able to preserve his conversation in an authentic and lively manner, which opinion the publick has confirmed, was the best encouragement for me to persevere in my purpose of producing the whole of my stores. (2)

At the end of this brief dedication, he confesses to a disappointment he suffered after the publication of the *Journal of the Tour to the Hebrides*, and how this disappointment will affect his biography of Johnson. In the *Journal* he chose to relate all interaction between himself and Johnson freely; "I was almost unboundedly open in my communications, and from my eagerness to display the wonderful fertility and readiness of Johnson's wit, freely shewed to the world its dexterity, even when I was myself the object of it" (2). However, he was criticized for being thick-skinned and unaware that he was the target of Johnson's rudeness. Such criticism forces Boswell to become more reserved in the biography. Although this reserve will not change the fact that he will "tell nothing but the truth," all will not be revealed. A subtle trick. I will not suggest that there is no truth in this display of hurt feelings; yet, I *will* suggest that it is a convenient excuse for leaving the reader in the dark if the need arises.

The advertisements to the first and second editions reflect the effusion of a man who has finally finished and published a long awaited work. Boswell is anxious to show himself to the world as an extremely conscientious biographer. This is the harbinger of the modern approach to biography that became extremely important as time went on, i.e. the attention to accuracy. Phrases like "I heard someone say" or "If I am not mistaken" which can be found in Johnson's biographies are strictly avoided by Boswell. He prides himself that he has "sometimes been obliged to run half over London, in order to fix a date correctly" (4). He attributes the late arrival of the book to

> the extraordinary zeal which has been shewn by distinguished persons in all quarters to supply [him] with additional information concerning its illustrious subject; resembling in this the grateful tribes of ancient nations, of which every individual was eager to throw a stone upon the grave of a departed Hero, and thus to share in the pious office of erecting an honourable monument to his memory. (4)

Here, Johnson is compared to the heroes of old. Where does that put Boswell? Boswell is the bard who tells the legendary story of the Hero to the coming generations: He is the keeper of the flame, the perpetuator of fame.

In the advertisements to both the first and the second editions, Boswell takes the opportunity again to prove to the reading public that he is the only person in temperament, connections, zeal, and ardour fit to take up such an immense project and to succeed. He adds the praise written to him by Reverend Dr. Adams of Oxford University, and he finishes with a self-advertisement:

> Such a sanction to my faculty of giving a just representation of Dr. Johnson I could not conceal. Nor will I suppress my satisfaction in the consciousness, that by recording so considerable a portion of the wisdom and wit of the 'the brightest

> ornament of the eighteenth century,' I have largely provided for the instruction and entertainment of mankind. (6)

In the last sentence of this statement one finds Boswell and Johnson's common outlook on the two basic functions of art in general and biography in particular, "instruction and entertainment" – the former taking precedence over the latter:

> His strong, clear, and animated enforcement of religion, morality, loyalty, and subordination, while it delights and improves the wise and the good, will, I trust, prove an effectual antidote to that detestable sophistry which has been lately imported from France, under the false name of Philosophy [...]. (7)

As we read the dedication and the advertisements, it is difficult not to feel the self-importance that manifests itself between the lines and sometimes even openly in statements such as: "Should there be any cold-blooded and morose mortals who really dislike this Book [...]" (7). However, we should not be too hasty in our judgement. In the "Advertisement to the Second Edition" Boswell admits candidly that he delights in his literary fame:

> There are some men, who have, or think they have, a very small share of vanity. Such may speak of their literary fame in a decorous style of diffidence. But I confess that I am so formed by nature and by habit, that to restrain the effusion of delight, on having obtained such fame, to me would be truly painful. Why then should I suppress it? Why 'out of the abundance of the heart' should I not speak? (8)

Perhaps here lies the reason why Johnson warmed towards this man from Scotland thirty years his junior. Boswell has an "open disposition" which was greatly admired and praised in the eighteenth century. It is, in a way, similar to the vanity, innocence and candidness that endears Jane Austen's Emma to us. He may not seem credible enough to write the life of a great writer and moralist, being a promiscuous "drunkard, and the whining, good-resolution type" (Nicolson 89). But he is always first to announce his weakness. As Harold Nicolson puts it, "there is nothing we can say against Boswell which he does not admit against himself" (90). This was probably what Johnson instantly saw in Boswell. After all, Johnson despised artful manners, indirectness, calculating dispositions. He would not have remained friends with Boswell if he had not seen through the love for attention, the vanity, and the whiny approach to life. We notice examples of this in Johnson's letters to him when Boswell becomes too indulgent in his melancholy, or too stubborn. Johnson feels a special affection for his friend who is capable of immense wonder and admiration which surely points to a generosity of spirit.

The advertisements in both editions are followed by *A Chronological Catalogue of the Prose Works of Samuel Johnson, LL.D.* since Boswell aims his biography to be not only a life-story but also a source of reference for Johnson scholarship. He takes pains to list Johnson's prose works chronologically. He divides them into two categories: The works that are acknowledged by Johnson, and the works that are "believed to be his from internal evidence" (10). His poems are not included on the grounds that they were "very numerous and in general short". However, Boswell does not forget to promise a reliable complete edition of the poems (which he never actually realized).

Boswell opens his narrative with a loaded sentence that comprises his admiration for Johnson, his tribute to him as the forerunner of biographical writing, his acknowledgment of the immensity of the work at hand, his self-doubt (in spite of his vanity), and his anticipation of criticism as a biographer:

> To write the Life of him who excelled all mankind in writing the lives of others, and who, whether we consider his extraordinary endowments, or his various works, has been

> equalled by few in any age, is an arduous, and may be reckoned in me a presumptuous task. (19)

If Boswell were to undertake a straightforward narrative, which consisted mainly of him telling – in story-like fashion – Johnson's life, the work would no doubt be easier. What constitutes the difficulty is the ordering and arrangement of the vast amount of biographical material which he gathered with "the scheme of writing his life constantly in view" (19). This consisted of Johnson's accounts of his early life written down during informal question and answer sessions, transcriptions of Johnson's conversations with him and others; the anecdotes, factual details, letters collected through research; and accounts Johnson passed on to Boswell through "the most liberal of communications by his friends" (19). The list makes it obvious that Boswell started from a point of maximum advantage for a biographer who personally knows his subject. The only faculty he needed to exercise, it seems, was his ability to stitch together the diverse material, and make the best of this biographer's heaven.

Before Boswell lets us see what he has done with the material, he turns to his major rival in the field, Sir John Hawkins, one of the founders of *The Literary Club*[2] and one of Johnson's executors after his death, who published *Life of Samuel Johnson* in 1787. Boswell goes out of his way to discredit him:

> Since my work was announced, several Lives and Memoirs of Dr. Johnson have been published, the most voluminous of which is one compiled for the booksellers of London, by Sir John Hawkins, Knight, a man, whom, during my long intimacy with Dr. Johnson, I never saw in his company, I think but once, and I am sure not above twice. Johnson might have esteemed him for his decent, religious demeanour, and his

[2] After a quarrel with the members, Hawkins left *The Club*. This earned him the name "unclubbable" as noted in the diaries of Fanny Burney.

> knowledge of books and literary history; but from the rigid formality of his manners, it is evident that they never could have lived together with companionable ease and familiarity; nor had Sir John Hawkins that nice perception which was necessary to mark the finer and less obvious parts of Johnson's character. (20)

Is Boswell right? And why does he take the trouble, at the very beginning of his biography, to attack Hawkins? Actually, Hawkins had more to offer than Boswell admitted or let himself believe. First of all, since Hawkins was Johnson's executor, he was named the "authentic" biographer by the press. He had access to fragments from Johnson's diary and papers (which he later showed to Boswell). What Hawkins lacked in charm and humour as far as narrative skills are concerned, he made up in penetrating observation and insight. His is less protective of his subject's image. He frankly writes about Johnson's marital discord and admits that he and his wife were even separated at one time, a fact supported by subsequent biographies. He also points out the strange living arrangements of Johnson with two widows. On both of these issues Boswell is silent. He does not go into the emotional and sexual complexities of Johnson's life.

Boswell is also angry with Hawkins for not paying much attention to him. "Hawky," he writes to a friend, "is no doubt very malevolent. Observe how he talks of me, as if quite unknown!" (Nicolson 7). When Hawkins refers to him simply as "Mr James Boswell, a native of Scotland," he reciprocated with "Mr John Hawkins, an attorney" (137). The fact that Hawkins was quicker in publishing his version was also disturbing to Boswell. As soon as his rival's *Life* came out Boswell issued a statement, saying that his version would soon be published and would be worth reading more than Hawkins's.

The other noteworthy rival biographer is Mrs Hester Lynch Thrale (later Piozzi) whom Boswell dismisses merely as "a lady who once lived in great intimacy with [Johnson]" (21). Her contribution to Johnsoniana is *Anecdotes of the Late Samuel Johnson* (1786). Mrs Thrale was indeed a very close friend of Johnson. She knew him through her husband Henry Thrale. During the time when Henry Thrale was alive, Johnson visited the couple as often as he liked, stayed and travelled with them. Johnson displayed a fun-loving, relaxed side of himself when he was with the extremely bright, vivacious Mrs Thrale. "With Thrale, he could behave differently, being by turns childlike, father-like, and suitorlike, his behaviour ranging from the confessional to the demanding, the burlesque to the passionate" (Parke 52). Mrs Thrale, like Boswell, was collecting anecdotes about Johnson. When Boswell heard this he wanted to see them. Of course, both were aware that they were "rivals for that great man" (Rogers xx). He volunteered to show her certain parts of the manuscript of the *Journal of the Tour to the Hebrides* in the hopes that she would show him some of the anecdotes. But it was in vain. To his great annoyance, Thrale also preceded Boswell with her anecdotes after Johnson's death, publishing them in 1786. It was so eagerly anticipated by the public that the edition was sold out on the day of publication (Rogers xxi).

Thrale calls her collection, which gives a lively presentation of Johnson in the domestic scene, "a mere candle-light picture". There is one anecdote in it that would particularly dismay Boswell, and help Thrale assert her own right to produce a book about Johnson. In one of their conversations, Mrs Thrale and Johnson discuss who would be Johnson's biographer. Johnson says that he would prefer Mrs Thrale and his old friend John Taylor to collaborate on such a project, or that he would do it himself "after outliving you all" (Piozzi 70). Boswell's name is not even mentioned.

Once the rival biographers are sorted out and dismissed, Boswell explains to the reader the guidelines of his method: He will choose not to talk always "in his own person," but will leave the stage to Johnson as much as possible. He will provide "whatever narrative is necessary to explain, connect, and supply" (22). The narrative will be held together by the skeleton of a year by year account. By the simultaneous presentation of conversations, letters, diary entries and the guidance of the narrative voice, the subject will be presented from different angles, "by which mankind are enabled as it were to see him live, and "'to live o'er each scene' with him, as he actually advanced through several stages of his life" (22). The primary material does produce the sense of immediacy – a lived life that is crucial to Boswell's biography. One particular sort of material – the recorded conversations – is mainly responsible for this effect. Boswell says that he considers the conversations as "the peculiar value of the following work" (23). His records of these conversations are sometimes criticized for being too detailed; but this mass of detail, as it accumulates, brings the reader closer to the subject. Boswell defends his detailed presentation of conversations: "I remain firm and confident in my opinion, that minute particulars are frequently characteristick, and always amusing, when they relate to the distinguished man" (25). Boswell does not neglect to show that his method is in line with Johnson's own ideas about biography. He quotes from Johnson's essay in *The Rambler* No: 60 and places himself within the evolving history of the genre as the follower of its most accomplished practitioner.

Thus, with the dedication, advertisements, and introduction the process of preparing legitimate grounds for the biography is completed, and with them Boswell builds a protective fortress around his narrative. Like a good rhetorician, he establishes authority, announces the support of illustrious figures, leans on the masters of the genre, anticipates and answers criticism and provides answers, establishes the worth of the amount of hard work that went into the writing of the text, and assumes the role of the friend-biographer who carries a great man to posterity. He hits the target especially in this last attempt: This biography *did* create the man until Johnson scholarship and interest in his works revived in the second half of the twentieth century.

The narrative starts with the date Wednesday 18 September 1709, the date of Johnson's birth. To get more information on his subject's childhood, Boswell visits Lichfield and interviews people who knew him and his family. Admitting that many of the details gathered there cannot be verified, he relates that he was told everything with careful reference to who said what to whom. Although the childhood sections will prove somewhat limp and weak for a post-Freudian reading, they are full of striking and sometimes endearing pictures: Dr Johnson in petticoats, Dr Johnson writing a little verse for the ducks, Dr Johnson being awarded some gingerbread for being a good student. Sentences full of "it was said" and "they told me" are put together to prove the precocity of young Sam Johnson (incidentally the title of a 1955 biography of Johnson by James L. Clifford). Boswell does not forget to add Johnson's warning to him that the talents of little children tend to get exaggerated by people who love them.

Young Johnson's intellectual progress, and his reading habits are also presented through reminiscences of school teachers and school friends. Boswell does not find his subject to have an ordered mind in his youth. He does not read according to plan and passes his time in "what [Johnson] thought idleness" (43). This "what he thought" is one of the first instances in the biography where Boswell feels the need to explain away the less than perfect aspects of his subject's character, and transforms what he thinks are faults or weaknesses into positive attributes. Johnson's disordered reading and study habits disturb Boswell. So, he first relates a vivid scene in which Johnson, thinking that his brother hid some apples behind a book shelf, comes across Petrarch, forgets about the apple and reads a great portion of the book right then and there. This anecdote is tied into Johnson's haphazard reading, which Boswell likens to the "grazing" of animals. And to the reader's surprise and delight, he connects the two with a comparison: since the meat of freely grazing animals is tastier than the meat of confined ones, the men who freely read whatever they want are enriched more than the ones confined in strict educational schemes!

As a biographer, Boswell finds it very hard to say anything remotely negative about his subject and uses a magic wand to transform error into virtue. Boswell does say that he intends to write "no panegyrick, which must be all praise, but his Life" and adds that "in every picture there should be shade as well as light" (22). However, the fair presentation of shade and light may not be always easy. A fundamental danger of being close to the subject is the distortion caused by the biographer's personal connection.

We come across the first instance of direct conversation in the sections covering Johnson's early life. At nineteen, Johnson goes to Pembroke College, Oxford. Boswell talks to Johnson about those years and quotes him directly on his irreverence to his tutor there. Suddenly the quotation turns into a dialogue presented as if in a play:

> BOSWELL: 'That, Sir, was great fortitude of mind.' JOHNSON: 'No, Sir; stark insensibility.' (45)

This surprises the reader. Furthermore, it gives the feeling that the written text is interrupted by an actual conversation in the room. This is something Boswell's readers get used to, and look forward to. One actually waits for one of these conversations to break into the narrative since the dialogues are some of the most interesting and amusing parts of the book.

We are also introduced to Johnson's melancholy in these early sections:

> Johnson, who was blest with all the powers of genius and understanding in a degree far above the ordinary state of human nature, was at the same time visited with a disorder so afflictive, that they, who know it by dire experience, will not envy his exalted endowments. (48)

As the narrative progresses and we read more of the letters between Boswell and Johnson, we learn that Boswell himself is one of those "who know it by dire experience." Suffering from depression, Boswell (in his perverted sense of pride when it comes to Johnson) seems to be proud that he shares this affliction with his subject. Proud or not, it is an asset for him as a biographer, because he can really empathize with Johnson, and his own affliction helps him to understand the man better. He knows that "to Johnson, whose supreme enjoyment was the exercise of his reason, the disturbance or obscuration of that faculty was the evil most to be dreaded" (49). But on the other hand, he uses this "melancholy aspect" to prove that he is showing shade as well as light. On other "shades" such as Johnson's prejudices or obscure relations with women, he is not forthcoming.

As Johnson tells the particulars of his early life to Boswell, he also relates his "religious progress" (50). Johnson's spiritual life, his piety and religious practices are important topics in terms of his moral life as well as constituting an example for the readers – given the biography's didactic aims. On these issues, he quotes extensively from Johnson's diaries and private prayers – which at times make the reader wince since they are of an extremely private nature.

At twenty-six Johnson gets married to Elizabeth Jervis Porter, a widow twenty years his senior. Boswell defines their wedding day as the "beginning of connubial felicity" (69). He depicts the marriage as one of perfect happiness and harmony, which other biographies, starting with Hawkins's, show as less than perfect – a source of unhappiness for both parties as the years progress. Boswell often displays Johnson's love for his wife through his prayers and meditations. These are mostly the occasions when Johnson thinks about his wife after her death amid feelings of guilt and repentance for duties unfulfilled. Boswell never taps into this problematic side of the marriage.

Johnson's professional life is less than satisfactory during these years. He works as a teacher, but he is not a good one, being short tempered and rash. Rather than saying that he was not equipped for this particular occupation, Boswell is willing to degrade a different type of talent required for teaching: "The truth, however, is, that he was not so well qualified for being a teacher of elements, and a conductor in learning by regular gradations, as men of inferior powers of mind" (70) or "Yet I am of opinion that the greatest abilities are not only not required for this office, but render a man less fit for it" (70).

The number of letters scattered among plain narrative increases as years go by. Suspense, one of the techniques Boswell uses extremely skilfully, is tied to his use of letters. Since letters add a sense of actuality, a "now"ness to the narrative, they help Boswell to push his readers forward by letting events unfold. For example, after introducing a letter he says, "We shall presently see what was done in consequence of the proposal which it contains" (78). The reader is invited to wonder about Johnson and what happens to him. The consequences of some of the events in these letters are also of interest to the reader, even when they are not directly related to Johnson. These events are of course topical. Most contemporary readers of Boswell's *Life* were ordinary members of the public who had no way of knowing what went on behind the scenes of certain public events. In this sense, letters provide interesting details whereby the reading public's attention is attracted and the borders of biography extended to something larger than a single individual's private history. This also shows how an individual's history can intertwine with the social history of the times and the place where the subject lives, in this case "the ocean of London" (76).

Boswell is not one to hide behind his subject (although he has a remarkable talent for disappearing when the occasion demands). At all times, we know who is telling the story, which may be partly the reason why this book is always referred to as "Boswell's *Johnson*." How the biographer is always looking over his subject's shoulder is well illustrated in a paragraph where Boswell talks about young Johnson's feelings when he first sees his name in print. He explains Johnson's feelings by using his own experiences. He underlines the fact that such an instance is a point of connection between the biographer and the subject. It is important for Boswell to let the reader know that he is able to find parallel feelings in himself. In this way, he is able to show that he can understand his subject's inner world. He stands next to the giant and shows how an ordinary person would measure up.

Since the biographer himself is such an integral part of the narrative, the reader eagerly awaits his first meeting with Johnson. Boswell was an admirer of Johnson and wished to be acquainted with him for the longest time. But the actual meeting itself is unplanned, totally accidental. The event is carefully dated in the biography as a landmark event like the Battle of Hastings or Waterloo would be. And the narration starts with an "at last," like a sigh of relief. On Monday the 16th of May 1763, Boswell goes to visit a bookseller's shop owned by Thomas Davies who happens to be a mutual friend. As they sit together after tea, Johnson makes a surprise entrance and they are introduced. Boswell does not come off very well at this first meeting:

> I was much agitated; and recollecting his prejudice against the Scotch, of which I heard much, I said to Davies, 'Don't tell where I come from.' – 'From Scotland," cried Davies roguishly. 'Mr. Johnson, (said I) I do indeed come from Scotland, but I cannot help it.' I am willing to flatter myself that I meant this as light pleasantry to sooth and conciliate him, and not as humiliating abasement at the expense of my country. But however that might be, this speech was somewhat unlucky; for with that quickness of wit for which he was so remarkable, he seized the expression 'come from Scotland,' which I used in the sense of being of that country, and, as if I had said that I had come away from it, or left it, retorted, 'That, Sir, I find, is what a great many of your countrymen cannot help.' This stroke stunned me a good deal [...]. (277)

After this exchange, Boswell makes the mistake of cutting into Johnson's conversation with Davies about Garrick. Chastised by Johnson, he lingers for a while, then leaves.

We learn from the footnote to the meeting that Boswell immediately starts keeping a record. He goes home and writes down "everything material that passed" in his diary. He writes the entry in plain terms, but later when it is time to rewrite it for the biography he makes it immediate and alive by the aid of dramatizing clauses and phrases such as "said he, with a stern look" or "cried Davies roguishly." In his diary entry he also notes down what Johnson says without "marking the questions and observations by which it was produced" (278). He transfers this strange amalgamation of comments to the biography in the form of a list without adding any connecting sentences.

This is an interesting and, at first glance, awkward practice. Throughout the work, one is often surprised at the sudden jumps from topic to topic, conversations, or letters introduced without clear transition. However, this disconnected presentation of heterogeneous material creates an impression specific to Boswell's biography that may perhaps be explained best in cinematographic terms.

Anecdote, letter, conversation, domestic scene, description and interpretation rapidly projected one after another create the illusion of a non-fragmented life, just as photographs projected rapidly onto the screen produce a sense of movement, of life. Boswell himself says in a letter to Bishop Percy: "It appears to me that mine is the best plan for biography that can be conceived; for my reader will as near as may be accompany Johnson in his progress, and as it were, see each scene as it happened" (*Correspondence* 2: 276).

Helped along by the optimistic courage of a twenty-three year old, Boswell is not brought down by the "mortification" of their first meeting. A few days later ("upon Tuesday the 24th of May") he pays him a visit at his home. Always aware of his surroundings and eager to add all the details to the picture, Boswell writes his first impressions of Johnson in his rooms:

> He received me very courteously; but, it must be confessed, that his apartment, and furniture, and morning dress, were sufficiently uncouth. His brown suit of clothes looked very rusty; he had on a little old shriveled unpowdered wig, which was too small for his head; his shirt-neck and knees of his

> breeches were loose; his black worsted stockings ill drawn up; and he had a pair of unbuckled shoes by way of slippers. But all these slovenly particularities were forgotten the moment that he began to talk. (281)

Yes, talk. The word casts its long shadow over the biography. Boswell persevered in recording Johnson's conversation all through their friendship and got better and better at it.[3]

> Let me here apologize for the imperfect manner in which I am obliged to exhibit Johnson's conversation at this period. In the early part of my acquaintance with him, I was so wrapt in admiration of his extraordinary colloquial talents, and so little accustomed to his peculiar mode of expression, that I found it extremely difficult to recollect and record his conversation with its genuine vigour and vivacity. In progress of time, when my mind was, as it were, strongly impregnated with the Johnsonian æther, I could, with much more facility and exactness, carry in my memory and commit to paper to exuberant variety of his wisdom and wit. (297)

He sometimes copies these notes exactly as they are in the form of a dialogue; sometimes he lists only Johnson's statements; at other times he announces a topic and lists under it fragments of Johnson's conversations written down at different times on this particular topic. He also gives his own opinions on certain issues, especially when he wants to delay certain information and to create a kind of suspense or tension in the text.

[3] He never used stenography or idiosyncratic shorthand as usually believed.

What he regrets most about these conversations seems to be the impossibility of recreating on paper Johnson's voice and manners but he tries his best:

> I cannot too frequently request of my readers, while they peruse my account of Johnson's conversation, to endeavour to keep in mind his deliberate and strong utterance. His mode of speaking was indeed very impressive; and I wish it could be preserved as musick is written, according to the very ingenious method of Mr. Steele, who has shewn how the recitation of Mr. Garrick, and other eminent speakers, might be transmitted to posterity in score. (599-600)

Boswell collects whatever material he can find and writes down all conversations he witnesses which are remarkable feats in themselves; however, something happens in this biography that is truly astounding and unique. Boswell encourages Johnson to talk when there is really no occasion: "Desirous of calling Johnson forth to talk, and exercise his wit, though I should myself be the object to it, I resolutely ventured to undertake the defence of convivial indulgence in wine, though he was not to-night in the most genial humour" (490). This seems negligible; but not so from the point of view of biography as a genre. Just the opposite. Boswell quits being just a biographer who witnesses what happens and records it for his work, and starts becoming an agent who actually generates conversation to write down. At first, he suggests certain topics that may interest his subject; but later he makes statements that he knows would make Johnson react strongly.

This may be considered somewhat innocent, but Boswell does not stop there. He tells Johnson what he hears about him from his friends or his enemies and records Johnson's amusement or anger. He then starts to contrive meetings between Johnson and certain people he thinks would induce interesting conversation for the biography. One of these is Johnson's meeting with General Paoli (409). Boswell hears Johnson talk against Corsicans and thinks it would be a good idea to bring him and Paoli together and record the sparks that come out of the meeting; moreover he takes great pride in his idea.

> They met with manly ease, mutually conscious of their own abilities, and of the abilities of each other. The General spoke Italian, and Dr Johnson English, and understood one another very well, with little aid of interpretation from me, in which I compared myself to an isthmus, which joins two great continents. (409)

Another arranged meeting, and maybe a more potentially dangerous one, is Boswell's carefully executed plan to bring Johnson together with a member of parliament, John Wilkes. This is an instance when one feels how strange a creature is Boswell the man and Boswell the biographer.

"My desire," he writes, "of being acquainted with celebrated men of every description, had made me, much about the same time, obtain an introduction to Dr. Samuel Johnson and to John Wilkes, Esq. Two men more different could perhaps not be selected out of all mankind" (764). He sounds like a collector of exotic animals. Boswell may be, in this moment, at his most interesting: An ordinary man who lives vicariously through eminent personages and who enjoys meddling with lives. Actually, here, he sees his subject almost as a research animal, and creates an artificial situation in which he tests his reactions:

> But I conceived an irresistible wish, if possible, to bring Dr. Johnson and Mr. Wilkes together. How to manage it, was a nice and difficult matter. [...] Notwithstanding the high veneration which I entertained for Dr. Johnson, I was sensible that he was sometimes a little actuated by the spirit of contradiction, and by means of that I hoped I should gain my point. I was persuaded that if I had come upon him with a direct proposal, [...] he would have flown into passion. (765)

So, he traps Johnson into going to a dinner to which Wilkes is also invited. He writes with excitement, "When I had him fairly seated in a hackney-coach with me, I exulted as much as a fortune-hunter who has got an heiress into a post-chaise with him to set out for Gretna-Green" (767). Johnson gets very uncomfortable when he arrives at the house ("he had some difficulty to restrain himself") but he acts very civilly. Then we come to a long section where the conversation is recorded in detail. The experimenter is jotting down the actions and reactions of the subject of his experiment. The evening is treated in its entirety rather than in short impressions, as Boswell savours the delights of his trap. He uses his talent for storytelling to the full and he *is* talented. The dinner ends without any confrontation, the two men get on well. All that is left for Boswell to do now is to remind us of how ingenious it was of him to get these two men together. As usual, he turns to higher authority for approval:

> "it would have been much to be regretted if they had been forever at a distance from each other. Mr. Burke gave me much credit for this successful *negociation*; and pleasantly said, that 'there was nothing to equal it in the whole history of the *Corps Diplomatique*" (776).

This is an astounding and twisted case of biography producing its own material or producing life. Can the biographer be any more "distanceless" from the subject?

After all the excitement and noise in the foregoing pages – the book does indeed give a sense of ceaseless succession of words – Johnson "expires" quietly:

> Having, as has been mentioned, made his will on the 8th and 9th of December, and settled all his worldly affaires, he languished till Monday, the 13th of that month, when he expired, about seven o'clock in the evening, with so little apparent

> pain that his attendants hardly perceived when his dissolution took place. (1392)

Boswell is not present. The account is given through a letter from John Byng to Edmond Malone, two friends of Johnson. When Boswell says, "I trust, I shall not be accused of affectation, when I declare, that I find myself unable to express all that I felt upon the loss of such a 'Guide, Philosopher, and Friend'" (1394), one does not doubt his sincerity. One overall impression the book generates is how dependent Boswell was on Johnson as a friend. Being a man who had a decided weakness for drink, a life-time sufferer of acute depression and a person ridden with debilitating self-doubt from time to time, he depended on Johnson for clear-headed comfort, companionship and most of all a sense of purpose. Gathering of material when Johnson was alive and putting that material together after his death filled Boswell's life. Practicing a profession that he hardly ever enjoyed, he poured his creative energy into this task. In a strange way, while Boswell recorded Johnson's life, Johnson created a life for Boswell who thereby carved for himself a special place in the world. Almost halfway through this colossal work, which oddly echoes the colossal presence of Johnson, Boswell wrote with reference to himself:

> A man who has been able to furnish a book, which has been approved by the world, has established himself as a respectable character in distant society, without any danger of having that character lessened by the observation of his weaknesses. (402)

Having completed his work on the biography and thus establishing himself as a respectable character, the biographer soon followed his subject to some unknowable world, no doubt in a hurry not to miss any of the conversations his friend may hold there.

2 Judas and The Frog Prince: Strachey's *Eminent Victorians* and Holroyd's *Lytton Strachey*

> Every great man nowadays has his disciples but it is always Judas who writes the biography.
>
> Oscar Wilde, *The Critic as Artist*

> Alix Strachey said there was something 'froglike and unfeeling' about [my biography]. This is my final attempt to change that frog into a prince.
>
> Michael Holroyd, *Lytton Strachey: The New Biography*

When it is historically impossible for a biographer to meet his/her subject, the main emphasis of the biography inevitably shifts onto a different axis. Neither Lytton Strachey nor Michael Holroyd had a chance to meet their subjects, and the two different directions into which they moved from that point illustrate the possibilities of the second category of biographies.

Before he wrote his biographical works *Eminent Victorians*, *Queen Victoria*, *Elizabeth and Essex*, and *Portraits in Miniature*, Lytton Strachey was slowly forming his own, soon to be quite revolutionary, ideas of what a biography should be. After his graduation from Cambridge University he wrote mainly reviews and essays. In 1912 he wrote an essay on Madame du Deffand which marked the beginning of his active interest in biography. He had read G. M. Trevelyan's biography of Garibaldi. "Yet he did not really enjoy [it]. It was old-fashioned, a simple hagiography without intimacy, celebrating the epic story of Italy's rise to nationhood as a liberal monarchy. 'There is much interest in it,' he informed Henry [Lamb] (15 February 1913), 'but tiresomely told'" (Holroyd 279). This quotation shows Strachey's two main ideas about biography: It should not be a hagiography, and it should be told with a certain style.

For his first biographical work Strachey initially picked twelve Victorians. He was a child of Victorian England, quite familiar with its imperialistic and often grotesque side through his father, General Sir Richard Strachey, and his crowded family of eccentric uncles and aunts. The approaching World War made Victorian England especially interesting to observe.

First he started working on the life of Cardinal Manning. He wrote to Lady Ottoline Morrell: "I am ... beginning a new experiment in the way of a short condensed biography of Cardinal Manning – written from a slightly cynical standpoint" (Holroyd 269). It was to be the beginning of a period of long and hard work. The biography was completed in January 1916. Virginia Woolf wrote to Strachey: "I have seldom enjoyed myself more than I did last night, reading Manning, [...]. In fact, I couldn't stop, and preserved some pages only by force of will to read after dinner. It is quite superb – It is far the best thing you have ever written, I believe – To begin with, what a miracle it is that such a group[1] should have existed – and then how divinely amusing and exciting and alive you make it. I command you to complete a whole series..."" (Holroyd 317).

In the finished version, which Strachey first thought of calling *Victorian Silhouettes* but later titled *Eminent Victorians*, the "whole series" consists of only four biographies: Henry Cardinal Manning, Florence Nightingale, Dr Thomas Arnold and General Charles Gordon. They are a carefully selected group of people, each representing a certain aspect of Victorianism; religion, humanitarianism, education and imperialism respectively. Although the title is ironic, it is a well-disguised sort of irony, parodying the titles of contemporary popular biographies. Biographies written around the time of *Eminent Victorians* quite often had similar titles given in all sincerity. The titles emphasized the respectability of the subject or subjects as well as the manner the biographies chose to represent them. When *Eminent Victorians* was published in 1918, many readers picked the book up in

[1] The group is the participants of the Oxford Movement, a revival of Catholic tendencies within the Church of England. Young Manning was influenced by them.

stores totally oblivious to the irony its title entailed, as the following words that Holroyd quotes from Hugh Kingsmill, "then a prisoner-of-war in his twenties" demonstrate: "I remember very vividly my first sight of it…the title *Eminent Victorians* caught my eye. 'I must examine this old bore,' I said, and made off with the book. That I assumed the title was unironic illuminates the state into which biography had fallen [...]" (Holroyd 419).

It would not take the readers long to realize that the book was breaking new ground. Strachey describes his approach in a brief preface, often called a manifesto for modern biographers. Instead of listing the names of his subjects, he opens with the difficulty of writing the history of the Victorian Age. This shows that his foremost consideration is to illuminate that particular time period as a historian. He writes: "It has been my purpose to illustrate rather than explain" (*Eminent Victorians* 9). "Explaining" can be done through "the direct method of scrupulous narration," but since he does not wish to explain, he requires a new method.

Strachey borrows from the terminology of combat, exploration, navigation, and experimental science to describe this new method. First of all, it is called "a subtler strategy." The subject is "attacked in unexpected places." "A sudden, revealing searchlight" is thrown to dark corners. Such an approach will produce a more impressionistic narration rather than a slow moving, detailed one. Also, the subjects picked are more like "specimen." The biographer is the "explorer of the past." He will "row out over that great ocean of material, and lower down into it, here and there, a little bucket, which will bring up to the light of day some characteristic specimen, from those far depths, to be examined with a careful curiosity" (9). The objects of curiosity – his four subjects – are picked as a means to give readers an impression of Victorianism; therefore, biography here is a means to an end. Strachey decides to use biography as his historical method because the genre straddles history and imaginative writing.

Although the first half of the preface suggests a strong emphasis on the work as a new handling of history, the second half shows Strachey's awareness of the idiosyncrasies of biography: "Human beings are too important to be treated as mere symptoms of the past. They have a value which is independent of any temporal processes – which is eternal, and must be felt for its own sake" (10). The statement reminds us of Dr Johnson's approach to the biographical subject. He or she has a unique being yet with a simultaneous universal appeal. Cardinal Manning, Florence Nightingale, Dr Arnold and General Gordon have to be presented in their unmistakable individuality but they can also be used as representative figures of a society and mind-set.

Strachey also reserves the traditional motive of the biographer, i.e. to document admiration for a subject. He wants to expose the "heroes" of an era for a new generation disappointed and frustrated by the false ideals symbolized by certain individuals. So, he picks his subjects as targets for attack.

His debt to the traditional biographies is that they teach him how *not* to write a biography:

> How many lessons are to be learnt from them! But it is hardly necessary to particularize. To preserve, for instance, a becoming brevity – a brevity which excludes everything that is redundant and nothing that is significant – that, surely, is the first duty of the biographer. The second, no less surely, is to maintain his own freedom of spirit. It is not his business to be complimentary; it is his business to lay bare the facts of the case, as he understands them. (10)

He strictly adheres to both in *Eminent Victorians*.

Strachey wrote the four biographies at a time when people who knew the subjects were still alive. However, he did not attempt to contact them or use their first-hand knowledge and impressions as source material. His sources for each biography are given in a short bibliography at the end of each section. These lists consist of published biographies and, if possible, letters of the subjects as well as memoirs, autobiographies or correspondence of people that surround each subject. He did not act as an investigative researcher-biographer, but chose to create what may be called a "second-hand" impression through already printed material.

His staying away from primary research, which is a point of pride among biographers, is consistent with his overall attitude towards the genre. After all, what did piling of details contribute to those tiresome volumes of Victorian biographies? It was not the facts themselves but how one presented them that was important. The interpretive force behind the facts was art:

> When Livy said that he would have made Pompey win the battle of Pharsalia, if the turn of the sentence had required it, he was not talking utter nonsense, but simply expressing an important truth in a highly paradoxical way, – that the first duty of a great historian is to be an artist. The function of art in history is something much more profound than mere decoration... Uninterpreted truth is useless as burned gold; and art is the great interpreter. (Strachey, *Spectatorial Essays* 13).

In fact, the quotation above carries Strachey's de-emphasizing of fact further. The quotation from Livy is a fake, one of what Strachey calls his "well-known pseudo-quotations" (qtd. in Holroyd 420). The quotation from Voltaire he uses as the concluding line of his preface to *Eminent Victorians* is also a pseudo-quotation: "Je n'impose rien; je ne propose rien; j'expose." Pseudo-quotations parody academic writing and its self-referentiality.

These jokes, so agreeably subversive of academic discipline, were examples of his oblique historical methods. He did not break with traditional narrative and create new forms as the modernists, Eliot and Pound, Yeats and Conrad, were doing. He used old forms but parodied the values they represented by inversion and pastiche, and undermined them with modern psychological innuendo (Holroyd 421).

The formal and contextual revisions Strachey made can be regarded as a demythologizing process. If biography is a form of modern myth-making (especially since Romanticism) Strachey reverses the mechanism. He starts with an attack on the religious evangelicalism of the Victorian Age. The biography of Cardinal Manning opens with a surprisingly commonplace sentence for so shocking a piece: "Henry Edward Manning was born in 1807 and died in 1892" (13). The lay readers of biography are prepared to expect saint-like lives when religious men and women are biographized. However, Cardinal Manning's life will not and indeed cannot be a hagiography because "[he] belonged to that class of eminent ecclesiastics – and it is by no means a small class – who have been distinguished less for saintliness and learning than for practical ability" (13). The worldliness of the religious figure is the area of scrutiny here. This worldliness entails personal ambition which Strachey seems to be specially disturbed by in all four of his subjects. He says that "it may be instructive, and even amusing to look a little more closely into the complexities of so curious a story" (14). This shows that Strachey's biographical foundation is still the traditional "instruct and delight" premise. Instruction still carries the moral tone of a Johnson biography, yet not so explicitly. Although Strachey is iconoclastic in certain respects, the fact that he chose to be an iconoclast implies a moral inclination. This moral inclination goes hand in hand with "amusing" the reader. Laughter is Strachey's most powerful weapon against what he criticizes. This laughter resembles that of a court jester, daring to expose, bringing out the truth, cutting inflated egos to size, and finally clearing the air.

The narrative does not dwell long on the childhood of the subject. However, the details are carefully chosen to introduce the environment into which the Cardinal was born, such as his father who is "content with nothing short of a bishop for the christening of his children" (15). He quotes the Cardinal himself on his childhood, than mocks his language. In this way, the reader never really sees him as an innocent child, sincerely in awe of the idea of God, but as an adult who heavily burdens his childhood with religious consciousness in retrospect.

Strachey lays open the fact that Manning's first choice was not the Church, i.e. he was not a man of vocation. According to Strachey "the thought disgusted [Manning]." Of course, this is not a fact but an interpretation posing as one. The word "disgust" is there as a tool of manipulation. Thus, Manning's later change of mind toward the Church becomes particularly suspect and insincere in the reader's mind. Consequently, it becomes easier for Strachey to underline ambition rather than a sense of vocation as Cardinal Manning's driving force.

Clarifying his stance against his subject thus, Strachey moves on to describe Manning's ascent to power: His nature is more suited to politics, and once he concludes that he does not have a chance in that area, he chooses the Church as a field where he can acquire similar power. In the backdrop to Manning's calculated climb to the top, the reader gets a chance to observe religious disputes at their most absurd. The endless doctrinaire arguments on what seems to be incredibly trivial detail, the effort and time devoted to such arguments by "serious" clergy is presented in a cynical and sometimes downright mocking tone.

Another important element of the backdrop is the depiction of other figures that Manning encounters. They are shown as having been used, wronged or even ruined by this fiercely ambitious man. One of them, Cardinal Newman, is particularly prominent. Very fond of using animal imagery, Strachey calls Manning "an eagle" and Newman "a dove." His depiction of Newman as a mild, deeply sincere, saintlike figure is often criticized; however, from the viewpoint of narrative strategy, it is an important clue for the Stracheyesque manipulation. All the characters included in the telling of Manning's life are included for the purpose of highlighting his negative qualities. Newman is made to act as a foil. The more Newman's innocence is underlined, the more calculating Manning appears. Even the short mention of

Manning's prematurely dead wife is there to reveal his dismissive attitude towards love and his having made a choice with clear conscience to enter into a marriage of convenience. Strachey uses the expression "the merciful removal" (19) for the death of Manning's wife.

Manning moves in a world of ugly political games. Intrigue and the clash between appearance and reality define this world. All too obviously, he is in his element here. The bustle and noise do not bother him. "All this worldly activity should not have been agreeable to a truly religious person," Strachey seems to say, comparing him with Dr. Errington: "As to Dr. Errington, he gave an example of humility and submission by at once withdrawing into a complete obscurity [...] He nursed no resentment in his heart, and, after a long and edifying life of peace and silence, he died in 1886, a professor of theology at Clifton" (68).

Pieces of narrative resonant with words like "humility," "submission," "peace," "silence" create pockets of tranquillity in the text by which the worldliness of Manning is thrown into relief.

Strachey is an energetic storyteller who supports his narrative by vivid images and dramatic passages. In a passage calculated to defy expectations, Strachey imagines Manning's audience with the Pope as quite an insignificant event, mentioned in Manning's diary with a mere "Audience today at the Vatican" (48). On another occasion, Strachey describes the Pope striking his breast with his fists, like an ape. Another time, he writes: "Cardinal Barnabo, Cardinal Reisach, Cardinal Antonelli, looked at [Manning] with their shrewd eyes and hard faces, while he poured into their ears – which, as he had already noticed with distress, were large and not too clean – his careful disquisitions" (70). While writing of a letter anxiously expected by Cardinal Newman, he adds the small detail of its being delivered in a blue envelope – which suddenly brings the moment vividness and immediacy. Other similar images are used again and again. They are part of Strachey's lively storytelling, yet they are more often than not at the expense of historical accuracy, which he sacrifices to impression and atmosphere.

The voice of the narrator dominates all four biographies and narrative authority is never left to the subjects. Whenever they get a chance to have their own voices heard through letters or diary entries they betray themselves because Strachey chooses to quote the voices at their most self-deceiving, contradictory, or ambitious moments. He says that Manning preached temperance. Surely, Manning had preached on many other topics, yet Strachey chooses to mention the one that would highlight the contrast between appearance and reality in Manning's life, given that Manning himself was an intemperate man.

Manning's life told in this cynical way fulfils its purpose. The reader is left with a sense that this man's great energy which could have been useful, was being misdirected and misused in the service of stark ambition. At the end, Strachey does not forget to mention Manning's "reluctance to die" (108). What is left behind from the Cardinal is, however, "a dim thing today." Strachey concludes that Manning's position in the Church hierarchy was all he really achieved, and with his death that came to an end. The image of the Cardinal's hat gathering dust symbolizes the futility of ambition according to Strachey. Towards the end of his life, Manning came to the realization that all the commotion in his life left no tangible legacy. Strachey chooses a quotation from his diaries showing Manning's self-deception. However, the narrative has already taught us to know deception when we see it in Manning's life:

> 'Mine has been a life of fifty years out of the world as Gladstone's has been in it. The work of his life in this world is manifest. I hope mine may be in the next. I suppose our Lord called me out of the world because He saw that I should lose my soul in it.' Clearly that was the explanation. (106)

The short remark following the quotation from Manning is loaded with meaning. Firstly, its ironic tone emphasizes Manning's self-deception. Secondly, it draws our attention to the remark "I should lose my soul in it." We know from the entire narrative that Manning nevertheless lost his soul, he was never really "out of the world." In this sense, the last remark is not ironic but literal.

* * *

The second subject in this quadruple anatomy of ambition is Florence Nightingale. In contrast to Cardinal Manning, Nightingale is indeed "in this world manifest" for she singlehandedly redefined a profession and greatly improved the health-care system of her country. The narrative starts with a direct, opinionated, striking and very readable paragraph, foregrounding Nightingale's well-known "Lady with the Lamp" image because Strachey will be working against it. Such Victorian images of self-sacrificing women are taken for granted, and Strachey wants his readership to reconsider them.

Nightingale appears to be a single-minded, determined young woman who tests the boundaries of what a woman from a rich, upper-class family can and cannot do. Her fierce drive is narrated in the same cynical tone as in the Manning biography, but slightly less vigorously. However, her struggle awakens the reader's feminist sensibility. Here the cynical tone does not produce the same effect as it does in Manning's case. It should be clarified however that Strachey's critical view is unconnected to gender – he focuses on extreme passion and ambition. As in Manning's biography, ambition is symbolized in the image of an eagle. Here is an imaginary scene created by Strachey to make his point:

> At times, indeed, among her intimates, Mrs. Nightingale [Florence Nightingale's mother] almost wept. 'We are ducks,' she said with tears in her eyes, 'who have hatched a wild swan.' But the poor lady was wrong; it was not a swan that they hatched, it was an eagle. (115)

Nightingale finds a place to exercise her knowledge and talent in a military hospital in Scutari during the Crimean War. War is presented as a means to an end in Nightingale's eyes. Strachey makes it sound as if she almost enjoyed the fact that such a grim occasion presented itself for her to make use of her ambition. As in Manning's case, Nightingale's belief that nursing is her vocation from God is mocked.

With a brilliant stroke, Strachey makes Manning and Nightingale cross paths through a letter he wrote to encourage her in her work in Scutari. After reading Manning's biography, this correspondence seems like two kindred spirits cheering each other on: "'God will keep you' he wrote, 'and my prayer for you will be that your one object of Worship, Pattern of Imitation, and source of consolation and strength may be the Sacred Heart of our Divine Lord'" (117). In the background, Strachey places the vivid description of wounded soldiers and the appalling failure of the English medical corps. These scenes show how little the government cared about the immediate needs of the fighting men who were sent to war with slogans of Victorian patriotism. Strachey uses sentimentality to drive home his point. Sentences like "There were moments, there were places, in the Barrack Hospital at Scutari, where the strongest hand was struck with trembling, and the boldest eye would turn away its gaze" (120) abound.

The way Nightingale fights with the incompetence of the health workers, the chaos of the auxiliary facilities, and the bureaucracy is told in a brisk style with short, abrupt sentences. The story is so well told that one wonders how Strachey is going to turn this example of immense personal courage and determination around and find something to criticize. Strachey's argument obviously is that Nightingale did all this for her personal glory rather than being motivated by a selfless urge to help others. In order to emphasize this he uses a patriarchal discourse – deliberately sentimental but meant to distance the reader with its vulgarity rather than stimulate warm feelings. Such discourse makes everything Nightingale does seem cheap and calculated. However, this manipulation is less effective on the reader than it was in the case of Manning's biography.

Nightingale's life after the war is more suitable for Strachey's argument. Her over-critical and mistrusting nature ("She could only see slackness and stupidity around her" [144]) makes the people she works with think less of the good she has done and more of the ways in which they can resist her authority. She disregards people and holds her mission above all else. Just as Manning has a foil in Newman, Nightingale has a foil in Sidney Herbert. Herbert is her ally throughout her struggle for the improvement of the health-care system of the War Office. He becomes Secretary of State for War, which greatly increases Nightingale's influence on the decisions taken. Strachey presents her as using Herbert's power shamelessly and frequently. As Cardinal Newman in the previous biography, he is depicted as a mild and merciful person, sharply contrasting with Nightingale in his lack of ambition. At the end, Herbert is spent; he decides to retire:

> The struggle was long and desperate; and, as it proceeded, it gradually became evident to Miss Nightingale that something was the matter with Sidney Herbert. What was it? His health, never very strong, was, he said, in danger of collapsing under the strain of work. But, after all, what is illness, when there is a War Office to be reorganized? Then he began to talk of retiring altogether from public life. The doctors were consulted, and declared that, above all things, what was necessary was rest. Was it possible that, at the last moment, the crowning wrath of Victory was to be snatched from her grasp? (148)

She even dominates Herbert's last moments. Strachey imagines his last words and creates an overly dramatized death scene:

> After having received the Eucharist, he had become perfectly calm, then almost unconscious, his lips were seen to be moving. Those about him bent down. 'Poor Florence! Poor Flor-

> ence!' They just caught. '...Our joint work...unfinished...tried to do...' And they could hear no more. (149)

Comparing her sometimes to a tigress and sometimes to a creature with tentacles, Strachey underlines Nightingale's destructive side:

> When the onward rush of a powerful spirit sweeps the weaker one to its destruction, the commonplaces of the moral judgments are better left unmade. If Miss Nightingale had been less ruthless Sidney Herbert would not have perished; but then, she would not have been Miss Nightingale. The force that created was the force that destroyed. It was her Demon that was responsible. (149)

So, in fact, Nightingale was responding only to her inner nature. Strachey creates a dramatic atmosphere where he turns everyone who tries to help her into insignificant, self-sacrificing and naïve creatures. With these poor souls around her, Nightingale grows old, and as she grows old, she creates her own legend. Her seclusion, signified by her "shaded chamber," weaves a web of mystery around the woman and turns her into a Victorian icon. She gets interested in philosophy and Strachey mocks her attempts at philosophy of religion – picks her most absurd arguments and restates them in a sarcastic tone:

> In some of her speculations, she seems hardly to distinguish between The Deity and The Drains. As one turns over these singular pages, one has the impression that Miss Nightingale has got the Almighty too in her clutches, and that, if He is not careful, she will kill Him with overwork. (154)

Or: "she felt towards Him as she might have felt towards a glorified sanitary engineer" (154). Among these mocking statements is a paragraph where Strachey tells the reader how Nightingale pauses her "instruction of the artisans" for a moment in her *Suggestions for Thought to the Searchers after Truth among the Artisans of England*

(1860), and talks about the status of women in society, "the falsities of family life," "the ineptitude of marriage, the emptiness of convention." In this paragraph, Strachey's sarcastic voice is silent; for once, he does not judge.

Despite the sparkle of its cool sarcasm, the reader is puzzled at the bitterness displayed towards the subject in this biography. Although the biography successfully criticizes the false humanitarianism of Victorian England, the attack on the subject herself is not fully justified. It sounds more like a personal disgust felt against those who possess active physical and mental strength – something Strachey lacked and envied in others giving way to his sarcastic and bitter attacks.

* * *

In the case of Dr Thomas Arnold of Rugby School, however, Strachey's fame in the art of debunking seems to be fully justified. The narrative of Arnold's life starts at the moment of his being suggested to the Board of Trustees of Rugby as a candidate for the headmastership. And it is hinted that he was chosen primarily for change's sake, by a group of people who were not sure what exactly that change should be. At his election he received "priest's orders," uniting in his person "religion" and "education." Here the narrative moves backwards to Arnold's childhood with a special emphasis on *his* education. One of the traits that Strachey will mock with particular emphasis, namely his self-importance, is found in germination in this early part of his life:

> It is true that, as a schoolboy, a certain pompousness in the style of his letters home suggested to the more clear-sighted among his relatives the possibility that young Thomas might grow up into a prig; but, after all, what else could be expected from a child who, at the age of three, had been presented by his father, as a reward for proficiency in his studies, with the twenty-four volumes of Smollett's *History of England?* (163)

When he was at Oxford University, there came a time when he had serious religious doubts. Strachey makes him meet and consult Keble, a man he talks about a great deal in Cardinal Manning's biography in the context of the Oxford Movement. Keble's advice to Arnold is very beneficial and he gets over his doubts quickly. Strachey takes this instance and juxtaposes it with Arnold's difficulty in getting up early: "His dislike of early rising amounted, we are told, 'almost to a constitutional infirmity'. This weakness too he overcame, yet not quite so successfully as his doubts upon the doctrine of the Trinity" (164). This juxtaposition reminds one of Alexander Pope's use of bathos. Strachey's technique dwarfs Arnold and mocks the sincerity of his beliefs.

Arnold's physical appearance could not escape Strachey. He says that Arnold's legs were "shorter than they should have been," a "fact" that annoyed Strachey's critics as much as the amount of "shade" in Florence Nightingale's bedroom. Strachey also uses this description to show Arnold as not-so-bright a man:

> His eyes were bright and large; they were also obviously honest. And yet – why was it? Was it in the lines of the mouth or the frown on the forehead? – it was hard to say, but it was unmistakable – there was a slightly puzzled look upon the face of Dr. Arnold. (165)

When Arnold became the headmaster of the Rugby School, the public schools were places where "license barbarism was mingled with daily and hourly study of the niceties of Ovidian verse" (166). Parents of the students did not care about the intellectual side of the education; their concern was primarily moral. Strachey quotes Squire Brown from *Tom Brown's School Days*: "I don't care a straw for Greek particles, or the digamma; no more does his mother. What is he sent to school for? ... If he'll only turn out a brave, helpful, truth-telling Englishman, and a Christian, that's all I want" (167). If so, Arnold is their man who will implement in Rugby School his own "reform." Keeping his subject's pomposity in the foreground Strachey says that Arnold "would treat the boys at Rugby as Jehovah had treated the Chosen People [...]" (168). Arnold supports corporal punishment. His subtle cruelty comes across in his joining of such punishment with future "promise of noble manhood." He devises a system where not only teachers but older pupils are "given the right to chastise" culprits (170).

Strachey points out Arnold's weakness as a teacher and claims that the curriculum devised by Arnold was short sighted. Arnold decides to make Greek and Latin the backbone of education simply because it is what he himself had studied: "if Greek and Latin had not been "given" [...] Dr. Arnold, who had spent his life acquiring those languages, might have discovered that he had acquired them in vain" (171). Strachey's Arnold is a man quite inadequate for the position of headmaster at a prestigious school. He hides behind his idea that knowledge can be safely sacrificed for other things. Natural sciences are not taught at the school.

His full powers are exhibited in the chapel during prayer and sermons. In these sections of the narrative, Strachey draws the picture of a pompous simpleton with a great deal of energy. He is full of unjustified self-importance. Since he is unable to judge himself properly, he pushes himself forth as one of the forerunners of educational reform and parents trust this man with their children's education. Consequently, the Victorian mentality prepares the new generation in the hollow, subjective manner exemplified in Arnold's character and educational philosophy.

In order to support his picture of Arnold's unscholarly attitude, Strachey states that he had condemned Strauss's *Leben Jesu* without reading it. Looking at the bibliographical list Strachey gives at the end of the biography, one can see that he did not use any source which would enable him to know whether Arnold really read the book or not. However, this probable pseudo-fact is a telling detail in Strachey's portrait of Arnold.

A second such detail is that Arnold did not appreciate music; a statement which brings Shakespeare to mind:

> The man that hath no music in himself,
> Nor is not moved with concord of sweet sounds,
> Is fit for treasons, stratagems, and spoils;
> The motions of his spirit are dull as night,
> And his affections dark as Erebus.
> Let no such man be trusted. (*The Merchant of Venice*, 5.1.83-88)

It seems to say in a subtle way that Arnold obviously lacked refinement and, most importantly, the ability to enjoy the pleasures of life. He occasionally listens to "'the Confirmation Hymn' of Dr. Hinds" (180); a statement which confirms that he is a boring prude in Strachey's eyes. Arnold's dull, colourless inner life is further emphasized through his lack of fondness for literature or any other art, and his lack of natural response to beauty.

Several entries during 1842 in Arnold's diary which he started to keep later in life, shows that he prides himself for working for the Glory of God. Instead of seeing innocence and potential in his young pupils, he is amazed at "[the] daily sight of so many young creatures in the hands of the Evil One" (181). He finds them to be unapologetic: "'It is very startling', he said, 'to see so much sin combined with so little sorrow'" (181). Through these expressions, Arnold emerges as a man who uses his position for personal gratification and self-justification without any genuine love and compassion for the young people he comes in contact with through his work.

Strachey's negative attitude towards Arnold is especially noteworthy. It is obvious that Strachey is puzzled as to how such a man as Arnold could be an educator. However, what he seems to be more puzzled about is how others, especially the parents, were taken in by him. He talks about an initial reaction to his "advanced religious views" at the beginning of his headmastership; but this does not last long. He shaped students in his own mold and they spread his fame. "He became a celebrity," Strachey writes, "he became at last a great man. Rugby prospered, its numbers rose higher than ever before" (184). In Strachey's view, Arnold is not a great man; he is imagined to be one by an admiring, sheepish public.

Arnold's death scene is made ridiculous, not through Strachey's effort but by his own words. He wakes up with a pain in his chest, and he says to his son "Thank God, Tom, for giving me this pain; I have suffered so little pain in my life that I feel it is very good for me" (186). And he dies. So, he lives and dies as a caricature.

The last two paragraphs of the biography briefly evaluate Arnold's achievement and come to the conclusion that there was none. He only worked to strengthen the status quo: "As it was, he threw the whole weight of his influence into the opposite scale, and the ancient system became more firmly established than ever" (187). There was an influence but it was misused; there was energy but it was negative.

Arnold was also influential in bringing about the worship of the athletes in schools, perhaps the only change he made in education; quite an annoying reality for Strachey himself who experienced it firsthand. The effects of inadequate schooling is inevitably far reaching; therefore, the harm done by Arnold cannot be as easily erased as, say, Cardinal Manning's. Of the four biographies, this is the only one which Strachey ends with a statement about the future, full of foreboding: "We shall see."

* * *

The last of the biographies is titled "The End of General Gordon." It starts like a novel with the manner and physical description of the General: "A solitary English gentleman [...] with a thick book under his arm [...] The singular person was General Gordon, and his book was the Holy Bible" (189).

The figure presented in this manner gives the impression of leading a life of retirement. After years of service, he seems ready to retire from active work. However, when a new opportunity of action presents itself he jumps at it. This choice triggers Strachey's imagination. How does a person choose the action, the violence and the turmoil of war and turns his back on peace and rest? Gordon, like the three subjects before him, makes a choice which appears curious to Strachey. He finds Gordon's life or rather how he ended his life of interest in two respects: Firstly, from the point of view of history, since his life is intricately "mingled with the frenzies of Empire and the doom of peoples" (189) and secondly, from a more personal point of view. It is a spectacle which would interest the "curious examiner of the past." "One catches a vision of strange characters, moved by mysterious impulses, interacting in queer complication, and hurrying at last – so it almost seems – like creatures in a puppet show to a predestined catastrophe" (190).

Similar to the structure of Arnold's biography, Strachey turns briefly to the childhood and younger years of General Gordon after the introductory paragraphs. According to Strachey, his subject showed a tendency towards physical violence and a dislike for authority early on in life. He fought in the Crimean War when he was twenty-one. His ardent religiousness never left him. This ties him with the other three subjects. After an attack of smallpox Gordon wrote: "'I am glad to say that this disease has brought me back to my Saviour, and I trust in future to be a better Christian than I have been hitherto'" (192). The bout of smallpox and the subsequent revival of religious feeling in Gordon are coupled by Strachey with an anecdote about a Chinese man who after an illness thinks himself to be the "younger brother of Jesus." This Chinese man later uses his religious "authority" to become the leader of a rebellious movement. He is Hong-siu-tsuen, the force behind the Taiping rebellion. Gordon also turned his religious zeal into military zeal. He was given the duty to suppress the Taiping rebellion. The parallel posited by Strachey shows Gordon's distance to the contemplative life. As in the three previous biographies, Strachey points to a subtle hypocrisy, a dividedness between appearance and reality, and a choice always on the side of worldly action and ambition.

He gives the reader a chance to see Gordon through someone else's eyes. He quotes from the *Memoirs of Li Hung Chang*. He does not forget to add a note to the bibliography that the authenticity of this *Memoir* is called into question. The Chinese man sees Gordon at his most glorious: "'What a sight for tired eyes,' he wrote, 'what an elixir for a heavy heart – to see this Englishman fight! ... If there is anything that I admire nearly as much as the superb scholarship of Tseng Kuo-fan it is the military qualities of this fine officer'" (195). This is an example how Gordon starts to turn into a legend in people's eyes. Typically after such exaltation, Strachey flips the other side of the coin: Gordon is also a reckless, arrogant, greedy man – "difficult to get on with." The subject's ambition is made very explicit by Strachey: "more than one observer declared that ambition was, in reality, the essential motive in his life – ambition, neither for wealth and titles, but for fame and influence, for the swaying of multitudes [...]" (200). His longing for glory makes him willing to accept a mission which actually is not suitable for his temperament. It is a mission which requires quite a lot of tact. The diplomatic decision to send Gordon to Sudan is used to reveal the intricacies of foreign policy and the myth of the enchanting East is attacked. Through Gordon, we are shown a glimpse of the true face of colonialism. At his headquarters Gordon puts up an Arabic saying, "God rules the hearts of all men." This is soon followed by a reference to Gordon's "intoxicated heart" (230). The intoxication implies both his powerful will to fame and his drinking.

Gordon's foil is Lord Hartington, who has a conscience, a true sense of responsibility, and is never self-seeking. But, even in Hartington's case, Strachey first praises him, and then attributes all his positive qualities to his dullness.

Gordon's last few days are narrated in vivid detail, like his hair suddenly turning white. His ambitious nature brings him closer to his death day by day. His life's legacy is destruction: "[it] had all ended very happily – in a glorious slaughter of 20,000 Arabs, a vast addition to the British Empire [...]" (266).

Strachey's economy of expression in all four biographies results in an axiomatic style. Such a style conveniently simplifies the facts; however, it also brings the particular traits of each personality into focus. Strachey does not try to explain, let alone justify the behaviour of the subjects. He does not try to make their lives coherent. In the introductory note to the 1986 Penguin edition of *Eminent Victorians*, Leon Edel explains Strachey's method and its relation to his use of irony:

> What Strachey understood, for all its abrasiveness, was the principle of human volatility; he knew that the ego seeks at all costs its basic defences; and he knew what other biographers had not learned – that a biographical subject is consistently ambiguous, irrational, inexplicable, self-contradicting; hence it truly lends itself to irony and to delicacies of insight and sentiment. (i)

What makes *Eminent Victorians* the biting, anti-heroic narrative that it is, is laughter. This laughter turn the all too respectable, stuffy, gloomy and finally hollow Victorianism into a grim joke. Strachey's aim is to subvert Victorianism through its four paragons and he uses laughter as his tool. Bertrand Russell was to record the following about the time he was reading *Eminent Victorians* in his cell in Brixton jail: "It caused me to laugh so loud that the officer came to my cell, saying I must remember that prison is a place of punishment" (qtd. in Holroyd 69). In *Eminent Victorians*, the biographer's narrative voice "take[s] over, appropriate[s], and silence[s] the subject" (Backscheider 19), inducing the same laughter in the reader. And that is Strachey's strength.

* * *

Biographer Michael Holroyd, who stands at a similar historical distance from his subject as Strachey, refuses "to take over, appropriate, and silence the subject"; on the contrary, his famous biography of Lytton Strachey turns the narrative over to multiple voices as often as possible. Holroyd is an English biographer known for his biographies of Hugh Kingsmill, Augustus John, and his four-volume biography of Bernard Shaw. The biography that will be discussed here is the most recent edition of Holroyd's *Lytton Strachey: A Critical Biography* originally published in 1967 and 1968 in two volumes. After the two-volume edition Holroyd revised and rearranged his material and published it in 1971, again in two volumes titled *Lytton Strachey: A Biography* and *Lytton Strachey and the Bloomsbury Group*. The 1994 edition "combines the contents of all previous editions, revised, rearranged and cut, with substantial new material added by the author." It is called *Lytton Strachey: The New Biography*.

Holroyd was born three years after Strachey's death. Many people who had known Strachey in different capacities were still alive when the young biographer embarked on the adventure of researching for his biography in 1962. What precedes the actual life-story of the subject in the biography is particularly significant. Since the time of Boswell, the biographers have felt the need for a space to talk about how they came to write the life of a particular person, to give hints about their material, to give an idea about the amount of work and care that went into the writing, and finally to justify the existence of the biography.

Holroyd's "Double Preface" shows us a side of biographical writing that is hardly ever witnessed in the centuries before: he talks about "being threatened with an action for libel for his biography of Hugh Kingsmill" (xi). So writing a biography can involve the author in litigation. This is especially true if s/he dares to write a biography while relatives and friends of the subject are still alive.

> Altogether, it was not a pleasant prospect. Yet my publisher, Martin Secker, who was nearing eighty, appeared to find the predicament wonderfully invigorating. It brought back to

> him, evidently, the good fighting days of D. H. Lawrence, Norman Douglas and early Compton MacKenzie, all of whom he had published! While the old man seemed splendidly rejuvenated, I, still in my twenties, tottered towards a nervous senility. (xi)

This danger zone is the territory biographers like Holroyd must tread. They have to make a choice between suppressing offensive material and using all available evidence and taking the consequences.

Holroyd enters this danger zone by deciding to write the biography of a member of the Bloomsbury Group who also happens to be a homosexual. However, these two points do not concern him directly in the beginning because he sets out to write "a re-evaluation of Strachey's place as a biographical historian" (xii). During his research he uses readily available published sources; but he comes "to the conclusion that Strachey was one of those non-fiction writers whose work was so personal that it could only be illuminated by some biographical commentary." This commentary could be found in Strachey's private letters, and there were a great number of them. Some were still in the hands of the surviving recipients, and a great many were under the protection of James Strachey, the author's brother. It would certainly not be easy to get to them. Clive Bell, a close friend of Strachey's articulates this point in one of his writings:

> But I am not a biographer, nor can, nor should, a biography of Lytton Strachey be attempted for many years to come. It can not be attempted till his letters have been published or at any rate made accessible, and his letters should not be published till those he cared for and those who thought he cared for them are dead. Most of his papers are luckily in safe and scholarly hands. (xii)

This is a declaration that ought to stop short any Strachey biographer-to-be, but the introduction is there to show how this particular biographer braves the obstacles and succeeds in the end.

Determined to continue his quest, Holroyd knocks at the door of the castle perilous. He is met by James Strachey himself looking much like his brother. He is the next best thing to actually meeting Strachey. The old man who meets Holroyd at the door is a replica, a shadow of Holroyd's subject:

> In a more subdued and somewhat less astringent form, he shared many of Lytton's qualities – his humour, his depth and ambiguity of silence, his rational turn of mind, his shy emotionalism and something of his predisposition to vertigo. As he opened the front door to me, swaying slightly, murmuring something I failed to overhear, I wondered for a moment whether he might be ill. I extended a hand, a gesture which might be interpreted either as a formality or an offer of assistance. But he retreated, and I followed him in. (xii)

This is good, solid story telling. The scene has immediacy, vividness, and in one stroke we get to see the outlines of James Strachey and – at a distance of Lytton Strachey. This is also retrospective writing. The young biographer will learn about the shared characteristics of the brothers much later, after reading the letters. However, in this scene Holroyd brings future knowledge and insight into the present moment, at the first flicker of an opportunity to get that insight. He brings the now and the future together – something he will continue to do in Strachey's life narrative.

In the house where James Strachey and his wife Alix seem to exist immersed in silence and in work (they were in the process of translating Freud's complete works into English at the time) with hardly any food, drink, or other creature comforts, Holroyd literally enters a chamber of treasures. James Strachey has saved anything and everything that belonged to his brother and there is more stored in the study.

The choice of an appropriate biographer depends upon a simple question: "Do you *still* want to write about Lytton?" asks James Strachey after showing Holroyd the immense pile of papers. The answer is yes, and forty-eight hours later Holroyd receives a letter assuring him of James Strachey's assistance. James Strachey has been "waiting for a time when civilized opinion had advanced far enough to make the revelations which these papers contained acceptable to public" (xv). It is now the sixties and "civilized opinion" is on its way.

The preface depicts how Holroyd gives the next five years of his life over to the life of another.

> Part of a biographer's research can have about it an inevitable sameness. When one has examined ten thousand letters, one may be forgiven for eyeing the next ten thousand with a certain lackluster. While I was examining Lytton's early and most plaintive correspondence, with its microscopic details of faulty digestion, neurasthenia, apathy, self-loathing and other unhappy qualities that made up what he termed 'the black period' of his life, I did feel seriously infected with many of the same ailments. [...] However, I soon became absorbed in this life, and over the years I was writing my book I do not think I was ever more than half aware of the outside world. (xvii)

The biographer, in a way, puts his own life on hold. His identity merges with another through empathy, and he draws closer to his subject. In the paragraph above, we note that Holroyd calls his subject by his first name.

The excitement of seeing the correspondence both by Strachey and other members of the Bloomsbury Group also comes through in this preface. Of course, being in the house where James Strachey lives, and working somewhat under his gaze also enhances the atmosphere of closeness between the biographer and his subject. Holroyd compares the excitement he feels to "the excitement of an archeological discovery" (xvii). The excavation is also a fight against time and destruction. Holroyd's episode with a dustman is quite symbolic in this context. He visits the Strachey family home in London to check if he can find anything of significance before the house is cleared by the new owners. As he goes through the basement, he sees dustmen taking trash out for burning. Holroyd gets into a tug-of-war with one of them for Strachey's bulky long-lost Fellowship dissertation on Warren Hastings (xviii). He also salvages a letter from Sigmund Freud to Lytton Strachey, "giving his thoughts on *Elizabeth and Essex*," a biography by Lytton Strachey. This scene also shows how vulnerable written documents are – a document invaluable for the biographer can disappear in a minute.

The preface is the place where Holroyd states his basic aims as a biographer:

> I wanted to accomplish four things – to provide a selection of the best of Strachey's letters; conduct a reappraisal of his work; present a panoramic view of Bloomsbury life; and write a modern biography. I would endeavour to shape all this into a conversation piece around the figure of Lytton Strachey. 'Discretion,' he had said, 'is not the better part of biography.' I should not be discreet. (xvi)

This last declaration, taking his subject and fellow biographer Strachey's approach to heart, is a fundamental component of this biography.

Once Holroyd gains the trust of James Strachey, Lytton Strachey's friends also behave generously towards him. He goes to see figures like Frances Partridge, Harold Nicolson and Bertrand Russell. Each meeting is delightfully narrated, with few but vivid detail such as Nicolson's sleeping with his eyes open or Russell's telling him slightly indecent stories of Oscar Wilde. Apart from these friends of Strachey, Holroyd corresponds with hundreds of people most of whom share what they know equally generously with this virtually unknown biographer whose motto for this biography is "not to be discreet."

And there is certainly material to be discreet about. Holroyd dives into the heart of the Bloomsbury Group where one meets with an abundance of homosexual and heterosexual love. The Sexual Offenses Act, which legitimized private homosexual acts between consenting adults, became law in 1967. Though no longer considered an offense, it was nevertheless difficult to write about homosexuality, which still carried a social stigma:

> I was setting out [...] to treat the whole subject of homosexuality openly – in the same way as I would have treated heterosexuality. But my plan depended on the cooperation of a band of mercurial octogenarians. It was for all of us a daunting prospect. 'Shall I be arrested?' one of them asked after reading through my transcript. And another, with pathos, exclaimed: 'When this comes out, they will never again allow me into Lord's'. (xix)

Bringing the homosexuality in the Bloomsbury Group and their friends out in the open should in no way be understood as an exposure. On the contrary, Holroyd is contributing to the realization of Strachey's implicit wish to bring this aspect of their lives "out of the closet." Holroyd points out:

> As Virginia Woolf indicated in her diary and letters, James Strachey believed that had his brother lived longer he would have turned what was implicit in his biographies into an explicit autobiographical campaign to achieve the same treatment under the law for homosexuality as for heterosexuality. I can see now, though I did not see it then, that he would have liked my biography to perform something of the work Lytton might have done between the 1930s and 1950s. (xxiii)

In this respect, the biography takes on a mission in social history. Homosexual love and sex is handled in the same matter of fact manner as heterosexual love and sex. This manner gives the taboo a normalcy and openness which it lacked in other narratives that reached a large readership. The narrative of Strachey's life tries to achieve what Strachey could not during his own lifetime. This is quite similar to what Dr Johnson tries to do in his *Life of Savage* at a more individualistic level.

The sense of drama we noted in the presentation of the meeting with James Strachey and with friends of Lytton Strachey, the entrance into the archives extends into the actual writing of the biography. This dramatization successfully raises the expectations of the readers:

> I had often been haunted by fears that I would not be able to do the book, that it was beyond me. Now these fears multiplied. I inched my way forward, writing in the mornings, typing or doing extra research work in the afternoon. This last section of the book took me almost a year to finish, and by the time I had done so, my two index fingers, the only ones I used for typing, were numb. (xx)

The final product, which is the result of such hard work, is presented to the approval of James Strachey. One of the main difficulties facing biographers writing at the time when relatives and friends of the subject are still alive is going through a series of authorizations before they are allowed to publish their work. In some cases, publication cannot be stopped; however, the use of certain important material can be prohibited. In Holroyd's case, James Strachey went through his typescript over a period of two and a half years (xxi). He made hundreds of corrections; but this proved to be a boon since the details of the typescript "provoked [him] into divulging all sorts of information known to almost no one else that would greatly enrich the biography" (xxi). So, this combined editing, proofreading and footnoting turned out to be a blessing in disguise. James disliked many parts of the book. Holroyd does not pretend that James liked one hundred percent of what he wrote; but he nevertheless makes the reader feel that, overall, James Strachey approved the biography. And that is the stamp of approval most biographers feel that they need to have.

> Readers of the biography might well deduce from some of the footnotes that James greatly disliked the book from beginning to end. He was never one to cover up opinions so that I knew it was true when he told me at the end he appreciated the seriousness of purpose and approved of the structure and length of the book [...]. Since I have never blindly accepted his opinions, and since I knew his approval was extremely hard to win, nothing could have pleased me more. (xxi)

As a twentieth century biographer, Holroyd is aware of the fact that a biographer who submits to pressure from close friends and relatives would be greatly suspect in readers' eyes. By the time Holroyd started writing biographies, unmediated facts became the foundation credible biographies stood upon. Therefore, the phrase "never blindly accepted his opinions" in the quotation above hails the modern biographer whose most important claim is to objectivity.

Here ends the first part of the "Double Preface." This is the preface written for the 1971 edition. What follows is a part added later for the 1994 edition. It is mainly concerned with reactions to the publication of the book. Of course, there are plenty, and not all of them good. What the selection shows is that the biography did indeed cause a stir. It generated anti-homosexual feelings; it was criticized for bringing out bitterness against the Bloomsbury Group by the relatives of the members. On the other hand, many homosexuals read it (as Holroyd learns from the letters he receives), and it brought on a change in the genre similar to what *Eminent Victorians* had done half a century before.

This is evident in Nigel Nicolson's own change of mind regarding the ethical guidelines to be followed by a biographer. When Holroyd's biography of Strachey first came out in 1967, Nigel Nicolson, the son of Harold Nicolson and Vita Sackville-West, wrote an article in *The*

Spectator to condemn the "indiscretion" in the book, he invited future subjects-to-be to caution when writing letters or keeping diaries. However, in 1973 Nicolson himself published his mother's autobiography in a now famous book called *Portrait of a Marriage*, revealing "his father's complaisance and his mother's sexual radicalism" (xxiv). Holroyd calls this "the barometric change in modern non-fiction" and implies that his biography of Lytton Strachey played a crucial role in that change. Holroyd relates various different opinions about his biography, especially through diary entries of individuals published after the book appeared. The private nature of these opinions and their ways of expression invest them with a sense of truth and sincerity, which in turn benefits Holroyd's image as an objective, truthful biographer.

Holroyd presents several solid justifications for a new edition: since the 1971 version, he has had a chance "to see and use more of [Leonard Woolf's and Lytton Strachey's] correspondence" (xxx). It is shorter than the 1971 edition with literary criticism of Lytton Strachey's own writings taken out of the biography; he has corrected factual errors by the help of the memoirs or other biographies published since 1971; he has had a chance to complete the missing side of correspondences in the triangular relationships of the Bloomsbury group, and he has done away with the pseudonyms entirely.

Holroyd's detached attitudes towards his subject were not universally appreciated. "Alix Strachey complained that, there was something 'froglike and unfeeling' about [the early chapters]" (xxxv). Holroyd declares that this last edition is his "final attempt to change that frog into a prince." Frog or prince, Holroyd's *Lytton Strachey: The New Biography* is the first attempt at objectivity among the biographies we have discussed so far.

After Strachey's slim volume of *Eminent Victorians*, Holroyd's bulky biography seems like a return to the Victorian biographical ideal in terms of size. It consists of four parts, seventeen chapters and an epilogue. The text is interspersed with three sets of illustrations. Such visual material has become a characteristic feature of modern biography. It supports the narrative and satisfies the curiosity of the visually oriented readership. Illustrations range from family photographs to individual or group photographs of friends, to photographs of houses, places, facsimiles of letters and reprints of artwork.

Each part and chapter has an epigraph related to the main theme of the following. As a post-Freudian biography writer, Holroyd devotes quite a substantial portion of the narrative to Strachey's childhood. He creates a very strong and distinctive sense of place while describing the house Strachey grew up in. It is an odd piece of architecture, stuffy, gloomy and full of shadows. The house is a metaphor for Victorianism which Strachey is to rebel against. It is majestic yet hollow and uncomfortable. It makes its inhabitants unhappy, sulky and sick. Poorly ventilated, it is like an ancient tomb.

The pater familias, General Richard Strachey, is depicted – after a brief mention of his background – at his weakest towards the end of his life. He is not the authoritative father one would expect in a Victorian general but a feeble old man reading novels and taking orders from a maid to go to bed. This central figure of the silent father is surrounded by what Holroyd calls "swarms of creatures in spectacles" (5). The uncles and aunts form an array of family oddities. Life at this family home is told in short, humorous sentences designed to identify each of its inhabitants with a brief note. The brothers and sisters are many and they all look alike. In this section of the narrative the family group, rather than Strachey as an individual is emphasized. It is like looking at a clutch of eggs and waiting to see one hatch. At last one does. The blur of bespectacled children with high-pitched voices come into focus and Lytton Strachey emerges as a "thin, pale boy" (13) whom his five-year-old brother calls "funny little creature" (23).

Holroyd parallels this young boy's love and hate relationships within the house with his aversion for Victorianism:

> Lancaster Gate, which became his personal symbol of Victorianism exuded security. Its grim recesses inspired in him an

> involuntary fascination he never outgrew. A strong awareness of this rationally objectionable heritage was early ingrained in him. The huge mansion gave off a faintly musty air of superannuated traditionalism; and many of the family embodied something antagonistic to youthful enjoyment. (20)

The images of the childhood home are accompanied by words like decay, decomposition and disintegration. Here, Strachey is also secluded from the masculine world. His older brothers are mostly away from home. Holroyd depicts Strachey's longing for male companionship through the image of a map he kept "for several years [...] on which he charted the movements of his brothers around the world" (19). At every stage of his narrative of Strachey's formative years he touches on a few details that might have later affected his sexual preference. Holroyd strictly avoids pseudo-psychology; does not interpret or try to explain; he is satisfied with hinting and letting the readers make their own judgments regarding Strachey's sexual development at this stage.

Strachey's education up to his days at Cambridge is told through two voices: the narrator's and Lytton Strachey's who had started keeping a diary. Holroyd often turns the narrative over to his subject. Through these two voices the reader experiences at first hand Strachey's newly forming prose style. It is a promising beautiful style, mature for his age. Especially in the entries on his travels in Egypt with his sister, he excels as an observant and amusing travel writer. The choice of integrating his childhood diary also serves another purpose. Holroyd gives us his teacher Henry Forde's opinion on Strachey's developing style: "'I do not mean merely fond of letters – that he is sure to be – but a contributor to them, a writer'" (23). This statement and the rest of his praise ring true thanks to the samples of young Strachey's writing which Holroyd provides. Most biographers cannot delve into their subjects' childhood because most subjects – including writers and poets – do not leave behind a juvenilia or childhood diaries. Therefore, in such biographies the biographers have to present the opinions of the adults who have read and evaluated the early burgeoning, without being able to present actual extracts. Holroyd uses this privilege very effectively.

Holroyd's efficient use of narrative is nowhere more visible than in these early chapters of the book. He writes in what one might call a "future oriented" manner. He presents the emotional and spatial atmosphere Strachey grew up in with a lens which helps us make sense of his future writings, especially *Eminent Victorians*. The same is true for sections about Strachey's education. Late Victorian political ideology as well as philosophy of education can be seen in a nutshell in a statement Holroyd chooses from the Abotsholme school prospectus: "'The aim is to provide an ideal home and life for the sons of parents who can afford to have the best for their boys' physical, mental, and moral welfare, and who realize that Education spells Empire'" (29). An excellent choice. Even such a brief glance at the school Strachey is sent to informs the reader about Strachey's future attitude to Dr. Arnold in *Eminent Victorians*.

Through his careful choice among letters and diary entries, Holroyd lets Strachey emerge as a character in his own narrative voice. At certain points, Strachey's and Holroyd's words are blended together seamlessly:

> By the autumn of 1845, Lytton had been made the head of his house. He was entitled to wear a tin mitre on his cap, to sport a walking stick, take roll calls and read the lesson in chapel – his maiden performance, from the First Epistle of Paul the Apostle to Timothy, being an exhortation to widows. 'The agility of my voice' he wrote to Philippa, 'is not particularly convenient in this respect; at one moment it is plunged in the depths below, and at the next is soaring with the lark at Heaven's gate – much to the alarm of the congregation.' (38)

This young boy of fifteen with the odd voice, with his tall and thin stature shows enough maturity to laugh at himself, and he is *not* a social outcast. Holroyd does not forget to point out the books that Strachey was reading during these years – and in this way, we get a sense of his intellectual development.

Holroyd handles the issue of Strachey's homosexuality openly from the age of sixteen onwards. He talks about the youth's admiration for boys and how this affects his future love life: "Lytton's infatuations at Leamington were platonic and inconclusive," he writes (40). This is a pointer towards the nature of some of his later relationships.

Holroyd does not explicitly talk of the physical aspect of Strachey' passion for boys. However, he revives a certain image in such an exquisite way that the reader is left without a doubt that physical desire is there: "His hero was a dashing young batsman, head of the avengers, a rather plump popular boy named George Underwood, very freckled and with red hair that dazzled Lytton during the bright summer months" (40). We know from the meticulously documented letters that Holroyd does not make up such detail, but he *chooses* not to present it through Lytton's own words. By doing so he distances the desire from Lytton and avoids being explicit. On the other hand, this marvellous depiction, fit for a novel (that red hair will show itself off to great advantage in sunshine) suddenly brings the text alive with physicality without being vulgar or overly intrusive.

Although Strachey is not an outcast, Holroyd shows that he feels lonely and angry at his own physical weakness. His first bouts of illness come when he is eight following the birth of his brother James. Holroyd interprets this as his means of getting attention. He sticks to this line of interpretation all through the narrative. He says that Lytton liked to play the role of the invalid and the victim. His inner maturation takes place despite or maybe because of this physical weakness:

> The type of boy to whom he was attracted tended to despise him, as indeed he despised himself, for being weak. When the infatuation faded, this contempt remained cold and real inside Lytton, reinforcing the agony of his own self-contempt, forming a fuel for his ambition. He remained outwardly timid as, inwardly, his spirit grew more anarchical and strong. (41)

This is an example of Holroyd's interpretation of what goes on in Strachey's psyche. These interpretive sections however are never designed to impose on the reader. The overall impression they generate is a sense of empathy and understanding on the biographer's part. The comments are never far-fetched or unconnected to what primary material shows. The tone is well informed yet detached. Even deductions of an emotional state are done through unemotional language. In sections about Strachey's love life, the sections most open to a sentimental, overly engagé interpretation or even, in a few instances, lamentation, Holroyd manages to keep his even tenor. Such a tone renders the narrative voice quite reliable. After a while the interpretation comes to be read not as the biographer's version of truth but as how thing really are, and that is the strength of well-written "objective" biography. The personal voice of the narrator disappears almost entirely; the neutral sounding voice becomes a presence that makes sense of the primary material. One handicap of such narration is that it creates a consistent picture of a life where almost all action, each stage of life moves towards a wholeness that does not exist in real life. Then again, this is one of the reasons biography is so well loved: because it gives a shape to life.

Strachey's sense of humour starts to be generally appreciated when he is at college: "'I have come to be considered a funny man, so that the audience began to laugh before I spoke'" (47). For Holroyd, it is not enough to present his subject as he is perceived and expressed by himself. He should be shown as others see him. For this purpose, he uses a great deal of material written about him. Often, a section of personal interpretation or Strachey's self-scrutiny is followed by someone's opinion or description of him. Holroyd seems to be holding a pair of binoculars and looking through it from both ends. The first lens brings Strachey closer, making the reader see his inner life, then all of a sudden, usually in a section divided by an asterisk from the previous one, he turns the binoculars around and lets us see him from a distance. This is a part of his overall strategy. The subject does not live in isolation, and a character can be, and in fact, is seen from two different perspectives, private and social. Such a look of course makes the picture feel more complete.

This two-pronged approach to character and events becomes more pronounced starting with Strachey's days in Cambridge. The previous chapters of the book come to the delightfully anticipatory end where Holroyd cuts off the narrative at the point of new promise – a new place where Strachey will actually come to his own.

For this new phase in Strachey's life, Holroyd picks a telling epigraph taken from a letter from Strachey to John Sheppard:

> Have you noticed that one's always waggling between two extremes – one's own opinion of oneself, and everyone else's? Sometimes I get so fascinated by the latter that I'm quite carried away and begin to act up to it, as if I really thought it true. We are all cupboards – with obvious outsides which may be either beautiful or ugly, or simple or elaborate, interesting or unassuming – but with insides mysteriously the same – the abodes of darkness, terror and skeletons. (56)

Although Strachey talks about the sameness of everyone's inner world in terms of its secret and unknowable aspect, that world is precisely what generates so much curiosity. Holroyd's access to the letters of Strachey's friends is put to utmost use from this point onwards. We understand through these letters that people did not know what to make of this new addition to Cambridge University. "The most usual reaction was to be more or less intrigued," writes Holroyd, "here was a new animal in their midst, alien yet inoffensive, whom it was not easy to accept and impossible to ignore" (57) As Strachey emerges from his initial loneliness in this new environment into a popularity of sorts, the narrative begins to get crowded with people – an effective parallel timely created by Holroyd. Most of Strachey's friends and acquaintances who come into the picture are soon to be well-known figures: Leonard Woolf, Clive Bell, Venessa and Virginia Stephen, Maynard Keynes, Bertrand Russell, G. E. Moore, E. M. Forster, Rupert Brooke and later Ludwig Wittgenstein.

Holroyd introduces these figures in two ways. First, he brings forward a diary entry or a reference in a letter about that particular person. Then he presents that person through a description written by himself, not through a quotation. The description, however is of course not solely Holroyd's, it is the summary of a number of references in the primary material, as in this description of Desmond MacCarthy:

> MacCarthy's reputation as a brilliant raconteur was partly rooted in his skill as a practiced listener. He achieved the feat of talking just enough to suggest a beguiling flow of storytelling and was at his best with people to whom he owed no special obligation. On these Saturday visits to Trinity, the apparent play of his soft Irish humour, the seeming grace and quickness of his speech, cast round him a haze of geniality. (68)

Once a certain character in Strachey's life is presented, his/her correspondence or, if available, his/her diary entries are used frequently. The members of the "Cambridge Conversazione Society" or the "Apostles" figure prominently in Strachey's life and Holroyd's narrative. Holroyd quotes extensively from the private papers of the members, enabling the reader to see what they think of one another. This is an intricate network of relationships and opinions. Among the correspondence used, Holroyd specifically highlights Strachey's and comments on the emerging patterns of his writing, for example his overcritical attitude:

> Forster was by no means the only person to be criticized in Lytton's correspondence. No one escapes. It is the writing of someone hypersensitive and insecure. Surrounded by many new friends, Lytton could never be certain that they liked him or be sure that he admired them for liking him. (70)

As Holroyd traces his subject's intellectual and emotional progress, we see the emerging new generation of British intellectuals in the background. These young men shape and test their ideas in debates. Some of the rituals of the Society or the topics of debate come across as ridiculous; there does not seem to be any effort on Holroyd's part to show them as such. Strachey stands out as the most interesting member of the Apostles. Then again, it is his voice that we hear most of the time, and this inevitably colours our impressions. Holroyd evaluates a speech Strachey makes in the Society:

> His meaning can be interpreted between the lines of his speeches and his idealization of the 'savage races' in 'Christ or Caliban' is offset by a vein of self-conscious humour. At the same time, the crusading spirit which follows through the speech is as real as Rousseau's call to mankind to throw off its chains and revert to primitive life. As real and as romanticized. Lytton did not have a truly speculative mind; he was not deeply interested in religious, philosophical or even historical theory. Yet, there is a force of feeling which thrusts its way through these lines – a belief in the freedom of the individual, his dignity, her rights. (79)

This last point seems to interest Holroyd the most. It is probably the same line of thought that draws his attention to the Bloomsbury group – the second group portrait the biography offers. Holroyd defines the group in his preface as a group that "helped to reduce the need for [pretences]" and seems fascinated by its openness. Holroyd certainly accumulated an immense amount of information about "Bloomsberries," as they were called by a friend. If he does not have information about a certain point Holroyd says "it is not known": "What transpired at Lytton's meeting with Sir Robert Morant is now not known" (74). We see here that the modern biographer cannot openly say "I do not know" as Johnson or Boswell were able to do. The modern biographer *feels obliged to* know. If something is not known, either no-one knows it or there is simply nothing to know, implying that if there were surely the modern biographer would know it!

As one reads on, especially the correspondence, one gets to know the people surrounding and in some cases influencing Strachey. Holroyd is there to welcome the reader into this world. For example, he breaks the code of the nicknames for us. He explains who had which nickname and why.

Each important event in Strachey's life is not only explained in the subject's own words, but also in the words of all the parties involved. This gives the events and especially the relationships solidity like that of an object. The letters allow the reader to walk around that object and see it from every possible angle. The network of correspondence carries with it a strong sense of gossip and intrigue. In order to keep up the suspense Holroyd does not reveal everything at once. For example, we follow Strachey's correspondence with both Duncan Grant (whom Strachey is in love with at the time) and Maynard Keynes (Strachey's confidant). Soon we are to learn that Grant and Keynes have been having an affair behind Strachey's back. We learn this at the same time as Strachey himself does in the narrative. Holroyd's timing enables us to sense the drama and also share in the overwhelming sense of shock and betrayal Strachey feels.

> Now that Lytton knew the truth, everything slipped into place. It had been he who, almost against their will, had driv-

> en them together. And to think that all the time he had been confiding to Maynard about Duncan's elusiveness, and joking with Duncan on the subject of Maynard's lack of passion, they could have been comparing notes. Then, too, while he was cautiously meditating on the relative merits of living with either Maynard or Duncan, they had gone off – so he now discovered – and found accommodation together in Belgrave Road. (181)

The sexual nature of many of the letters sent by Lytton and his friends are described simply in general terms; Holroyd never quotes directly from them. As Richard Ellmann says in his *Golden Codgers*, "we have savoured the emotional convolutions of Lytton Strachey's love life with Carrington and their friends, but the precise anatomical convolutions remain shrouded by the last rags of biographical decorum" (4). We should not forget that the letter writers were committing a crime under the English law at the time.

Holroyd also juxtaposes contradictory ideas about a character in order to attain a fuller picture. He does the same with certain events. He uses his "future oriented" method in these contexts as well. If a certain character or event will have a bearing on a future one, or if there are analogies to be drawn, he says so then and there. He occasionally hovers over Strachey's life and reaches and pulls out parts of the future relevant to the present moment. In the following example he wonders what sort of shape Strachey's desires would take, so he lets us take a peek into the future for a second:

> Once he had established himself as a writer, the direction, though not the nature, of his desires would change, aiming once more for the impossible. After *Eminent Victorians* he would again worship blue-eyed rowing Blues and handsome young Old Etonians. But those days were still far off. (131)

These rare glimpses into the future do not at all weaken the sense of present that dominates the narrative. The present is enhanced by the use of letters, which tell us about events as they are taking place. And Strachey's life unfolds through this "now." Letters reveal so much of the private thoughts of Strachey and his friends that one can not help thinking how difficult it must have been for the ones who were left behind to read this biography. They probably learned what others actually thought about them for the first time. It must have been especially painful that the offensive, negative, or hurtful words came from the letters of a person long dead and there was no chance of reconciliation.

Although the Bloomsbury group embodied the ideas of openness and sexual freedom, an atmosphere of loneliness, mistrust, and pain oozes from the letters. Page after page of nerve-racking claustrophobic relationships enhance this sense. Holroyd's own interpretation is absent from the narrative in such instances – the silence turning into an attitude in itself. The bickering, the complaining, the betrayal going on for years and years is annoying at times. "The Bloomsberries" belong to that class which can and does live a life of leisure. The careful reader may sense a personal reaction against them in Holroyd's subtle use of irony, for example when he says that "[t]he problems were endless" (159) – when the issue is choosing a place to go for a leisurely reading-party at Easter.

A change in Holroyd's cool detachment coincides with Strachey's leaving behind his somewhat egotistical existence and becoming an, albeit slight, influence on the social consciousness of the age. Bloomsbury also has its share in this change. The world starts turning into a place where one can say what one means. "The growing informality of these friends was to be seen as a contribution to the changing social history," Holroyd writes (171). The narrative voice assumes a respectful tone and loses its reticence when he talks about Strachey's evolution away from his ego towards the outside world.

The second area where the narrative voice sounds more respectful and involved is Strachey's literary output. Although Holroyd cut the literary criticism out into another volume in the 1971 edition, and left it out completely for the 1994 edition, still Strachey's writings and especially his three biographies are traced from their germination as ideas in Strachey's mind to their reverberations in the literary world. The connection between each work and Strachey's private, especially emotional, life are carefully drawn. Each receives a section where contemporary critical reactions are detailed and evaluated. Holroyd does this in order to "re-evaluate Strachey's place as a biographical historian" (xii).

Holroyd does not use humour in the same way Strachey does in *Eminent Victorians*. He uses it not to debunk, but simply to show the place of humour in the life of Strachey and his friends. The narrative has its own jokes such as short repeated phrases or the queer remarks of an old lady. These small opportunities to draw a smile are essential in a narrative of this length. Although Holroyd is not a humorous or ironic writer, he is fully capable of recognizing and appreciating the two where Strachey is concerned. This can be easily understood from his spot on selections of the examples of Strachey's wit, sense of humour and biting irony.

As a biographer Holroyd is also very familiar with the Stracheyesque style of writing. He has absorbed his subject's style to such an extent that in certain places his own voice merges with Strachey's, and it is difficult to decide who is speaking, such as in his description of Stonehenge written in the same flavour as Strachey's travel writings (266). In other places his humour seems to simulate Strachey's (244).

Holroyd's confidence in the strength of authentic voices in rendering crucial scenes is nowhere more evident than in Strachey's death scene. Here the source is primarily Strachey's long time partner Dora Carrington's diary. Pippa Strachey (his sister), Frances and Ralph Partridge are also with her. Strachey's room, the ensuing silence and its "surreal immobility" are beautifully evoked by the narrative voice. Holroyd does not quote from Carrington's diary at first. As the moment of Strachey's death nears, Holroyd turns the narrative over first to Ralph, then to Frances very briefly and finally to Carrington, who adores Lytton Strachey and kills herself shortly after his death.

> Ralph took Frances up to see [Carrington] 'still very white, but with the hectic colour in her cheeks that comes from inhaling gas.'[2] They kissed and Frances 'felt the thick softness of her hair against [her] cheek'. At midday she got up and went into Lytton's room. He was still sleeping, breathing deeply and fast. Pippa sat near his bed. 'I went up and sat in a chair, and watched him,' Carrington wrote. '"So this is death" I kept on saying to myself.' (682)

Here, just like the red hair of a beloved in the sunshine, the seemingly small detail of how Carrington's hair feels on Frances's cheek may be one of the most brilliant little touches in the book. It makes the reality of the scene rush to one's senses. The paragraph that follows the quotation above is the last paragraph of Lytton Strachey's narrative and it is entirely in his beloved Carrington's words – another exquisite choice.

But the book does not end there. Holroyd has been criticized for not finishing the book at Strachey's death, but going on with an epilogue. This criticism is groundless, since the epilogue does not stand detached from the narrative and is not superfluous. In fact, it is crucial in depicting the huge gap Strachey left in the lives of the people around him, especially that of Dora Carrington, whose attachment to him permeated her whole being, so much so that she could not go on after Strachey's death. The quotations from her private "Book" are es-

---

[2] Carrington's first attempt to kill herself was during Lytton Strachey's last illness.

pecially relevant here – a firsthand account of her feelings expressed by poignant simplicity and rawness. And finally she describes Strachey as someone to whom she never needed to lie. These words throw light on the whole biography, because they immediately bring Strachey's hallmark humour to mind: as Holroyd himself said in his introduction to *Eminent Victorians*, "humour of this quality is *an instinct for truth* as well as a weapon against all forms of despotism" (xii). Strachey's humour drives away the lies, both the lies surrounding his biographical subjects and the lies in his private life. Like a jester, he clears the air.

3 Too Far For Comfort: Honan's *Jane Austen, Her Life* and Motion's *Keats*

> [...] when people are dead, the truth is the biggest tribute you can pay to them.
>
> Claire Tomalin, *Interview with Jane Sullivan*

What about those biographers who do not even have a chance to meet the relatives or friends of their subjects? Many biographers writing today are in this category. Being historically distanced from one's subject, in some cases by hundreds of years, carries with it the lack of all the advantages discussed in the previous chapters. However, it has one substantial advantage: freedom. A biographer writing a life lived many generations ago is almost never burdened by family authorization. There is no one who might be directly offended or seriously hurt by anything that may be written in the biography. There might be great-granddaughters, nephews, or a large group of devoted admirers; but they cannot be compared to an angry husband threatening to sue or a son preventing the publication of the product of years and years of arduous work. The available material can be freely used; the field of interpretation is open.

In order to look at the narrative strategies employed in biographies which enjoy the freedom afforded by distance, let us look at the works of two contemporary biographers: Park Honan's 1987 biography of Jane Austen and Andrew Motion's 1997 biography of John Keats. Honan is also known for his biographical works on Robert Browning, Matthew Arnold, William Shakespeare, and Christopher Marlowe. Motion, on the other hand, wrote the lives of the Lamberts and Philip Larkin.

One problem faced by contemporary biographers writing about the distant past is competition. Most of the subjects are well-known figures in literature, performing arts, politics, sports etc. A personal interest, a revival of the works, or any other legacy, even a publisher's offer may be the biographer's starting point. Unfortunately, the biographer is seldom the first one attempting to write that particular subject's life. Consequently, s/he needs a justification for yet another biography of the same subject.

A better example can hardly be found for this than the biographer-subject pair Park Honan-Jane Austen. There are already several Jane Austen biographies on the bookshelves. Is there a need for a new one? Why should readers pick Honan's biography and not any other? Anticipating and responding to such questions are the responsibility of both the biographer and the publisher.

The publisher's response can be read on the back and front as well as on the folds of the book-jacket. On the cover of Honan's *Jane Austen, Her Life* a reader finds two reassurances. The first is the expression "Definitive Portrait," a derivative of the more common "Definitive Biography." This biography is claimed to be "The Definitive Portrait of Jane Austen. Her Life, Her Art, Her Family, Her World." So you may find whatever you are looking for in this biography. Since this is the definitive version, the reader will not need to buy any other biography written before or to be written after. The second reassurance consists of comments made by critics. The cover features two: "The best biography Jane Austen has ever received" by *Newsweek* and "A triumph ... the only biography of Austen that she would have liked" by the *Philadelphia Inquirer*. Four additional comments are placed on the first page, preceding the title page. Such advertising brings contemporary movie advertising to mind. This points to the fact that biography, like film, is a consumer item of popular culture and the consumer needs advice about the product.

Once the reader gets past the publisher's justifications, it is the biographer's turn to present himself with a somewhat more substantial justification. This justification is almost always given in a preface and Honan's is no exception:

> Jane Austen is the subject of so much attention, each year, that one must be very clear about one's aims in offering a new biography of this length.
>
> The last study based on most of the Austen family manuscripts is the *Life and Letters*, published by W. and R. A. Austen-Leigh in 1913. *No biography has taken account* of a wealth of Austen family manuscripts that has turned up since; also, *new data from research emerges year by year*, and not since Elizabeth Jenkins's attractive study in 1938 has anyone *seriously* tried to assimilate it.
>
> My aim is to show Jane Austen's life as *intimately* and *completely* as our new data and the rich, existing manuscript material will allow. (Preface, n. pag.; emphases mine)

Honan's "new material" is family manuscripts, which means that actually no personal material directly related to Austen was discovered. This is a widely known fact. No drafts of a novel, no diary, or personal letters have recently been found. What Honan points out as the major difference between his biography and the ones written before is peripheral material. I do not mean to disparage such new evidence; however, I should emphasize that Honan's find cannot be compared to what Michael Holroyd comes across in James Strachey's house.

Others got there before Honan did, simply because of the historical distance between him and his subject. Holroyd was looking for material only twenty-seven years after his subject's death, and Honan after a hundred and seventy years. The above quotation from Honan's preface never actually claims that the new material was not used by other biographers, it just says that it was not used "seriously." So, here are the three key terms to Honan's version: seriousness, intimacy and completeness. No small claim. Some of the material he mentions was indeed first seen by Honan himself. And his story of discovery is as exciting as Holroyd's. But we cannot find this story in the biography itself. For that story we must turn to another, a later book by Honan, *Author's Lives: On Literary Biography and the Arts of Language*. There Honan talks about how a couple, "one, a direct descendant of the eighteenth-century Austens," without being aware, presents him with letters. Here is a short extract:

> One Sunday afternoon, my hostess said in effect, "[...] I recall something that was put in the attic when we married long ago. Would you mind helping me look for it upstairs?" Upstairs we went. Under old carpets, we found a trunk, and a third and fourth key opened it; it seemed filled to the brim with eighteen-century holograph letters. (xvi)

They turned out to be "a good portion of the surviving Austen family letters." What were Honan's reasons for leaving this out of the preface to his biography? The risk of sounding very much like the famous Holroyd? An acknowledgement that this scene did not have an immediate bearing on Jane Austen's life? A consciousness that not a single one of the letters belonged to Austen herself?

In fact, Honan's choice of leaving the personal detective work out of the book carries a more important function though. It is a clue to his biographical emphasis and consequently, his style. He is not concerned with foregrounding his own "relationship" with his subject. His primary interest is in the "reconstruction of a picture" in which the subject is at the centre. In Jane Austen's case, there is more biographical material available about people surrounding her than material that immediately pertains to her. Honan uses this very much to his advantage in his biography of Austen.[1] He provides a social context around his subject made of all the available personal, familial, and historical

[1] His use of the same approach in his 1998 biography of Shakespeare is less successful. Abundant information on Shakespeare's hometown, his neighbours, and London yoked together cannot hide the meagreness of solid evidence on Shakespeare's life – if nothing else, it makes it more glaringly obvious.

material. He shows us Austen's world through the eyes of everyone around her so that one, more or less, sees how the subject herself is informed. In doing this, he gets help from fiction, and being someone who lives and writes for an age dominated by visual images, from cinema. Such a reconstruction is essential for both the biographer and the reader. The age in which the subject lives should be presented thoroughly for a better understanding and evaluation of character, mood, emotion, reaction, and action. The readers cannot be expected to do this without the help of the biographer, since they are neither contemporaries nor near contemporaries of the subject, nor are they scholars of the period in question.

The biography opens with "Prelude: Frank Austen's Ride Home." Other chapters have similar titles reminding one of chapter headings from novels: "Lady from France," "I Could Have Died of Laughter," "After Midnight," "Dancing in Kent," "Nelson Relaxes." "Prelude," the first of these, is written in the third person but follows Frank Austen's (Jane Austen's youngest brother but one) gaze upon the world around him. Frank's diaries, letters home during his naval training in Portsmouth and "other sources," Honan tells us, "help us to reconstruct a picture of England outside Steventon in Jane Austen's childhood" (1). The actual biographical facts conveyed in this chapter are the following:

1. Frank Austen was Jane Austen's older brother by twenty months.
2. He went to be trained as a midshipman at the Royal Academy of the Navy in Portsmouth.
3. He was ten years old at the time.
4. He left a detailed account of his years there.
5. He was allowed to go home for the holidays.
6. He travelled by coach most of the way, then briefly walked the rest.

Instead of stating these facts and quoting from Frank's account, Honan starts a third person narrative directly informed by Frank's writings: "Let us begin at Portsmouth and follow Frank on a ride home" (1): a statement full of promise – promising participation and drawing the readers into a cinematographic narrative. The camera first looks at a group of young trainees rowing out to an anchored ship, then singles Frank out. Colours abound: "the black, gold, orange, yellow and silver beakheads of the warships" (1), "black greasy ropes," "bright red bulkheads," "rose-coloured building" (2). Next to these visually stimulating images are put striking and gory details: The bulkheads are painted red because "red paint conceals blood," or a wounded boy "bite[s] into a leather gag as his leg [is] cut off" (2).

These are of course conscious choices on Honan's part. This harsher side of life does not appear in Austen's novels, which led many to believe that she was oblivious to it. By contrast, Honan and other contemporary biographers of Austen want to show how war, revolution, social imbalance, and injustice were quite within her domain. She was not the secluded, uninformed genius that people imagined. Therefore, it is essential in Honan's biography that people surrounding Austen are shown as participating in different walks of life, communicating their knowledge either directly to her or to other members of the same household. To serve this purpose, the family writings are used very effectively by Honan. In this way, Honan accounts for Austen's familiarity with what was going on in England and indeed in the world,[2] familiarity which shows up in the subtle unrest that makes itself felt in her novels in increasing doses towards the end of her life. This means that Honan also serves the critical side of the biography by trying to hold the circumference of the biographical field as wide as possible.

Honan wants the reader to participate in the creation of Austen's world through the use of association. In this sense the "Prelude" is a

---

[2] Austen had a cousin who first lived in India in close contact with the household of Warren Hastings and later lost an aristocrat husband to the guillotine during the French revolution. She also had another sailor brother besides Frank who fought and travelled around the world, and yet another brother who worked in London. Her aunt was arrested for stealing and almost sent to Australia on a ship of convicts.

presentation of Honan's aims and provides a guideline as to how the reader should utilize the information in the biography. For instance, Frank "keeps a very neat Plan of his training notes" (2). This should be associated with his sister's habit of neatness. The sailors on board ship drink a "fiery white wine" called *mistella*, more popularly known as "Miss Taylor" among the soldiers (3). This should later reverberate in our minds as the Miss Taylor of *Emma*. On his way home, Frank passes through Wickham, and there "Frank was not far from an arrogant James D'Arcy whose name became a scandal" (5) – of course the place and person names should bring an echo of *Pride and Prejudice* to our minds. These names, places, events, mostly excavated through reading of peripheral material, may or may not have anything to do with Austen's later choices in her novels. However, Honan does something which I find to be unique among biography writers: He seems to want to create a subconscious area of associations, connotations, and reverberations similar to Austen's own. And this difficult yet quite rewarding endeavour works well for this particular biography.

Little Frank Austen comes home. And as the opening sentence promises, we do follow him with our eyes and other senses as far as the text allows. Besides the social setting, the depiction of the physical look and feel of late eighteenth century Hampshire is also important for Honan as a part of his recreation of Austen's environment. "Bronze and white flecked" fields (7), elm and beech trees, the swallows, swifts and martins all have their place in this picture. "The sounds of horses' hooves clattering by on the flint" (7) brings us back to the coach Frank travels in.

> Frank left his coach at the inn where his sisters often collected the post, and then passed the white cottages. The lane here was overhung with greenery and so narrow that a coachman might complain of having varnish scratched off. In the Navy Frank tried to control his feelings, though his sister Jane nev-

> er found him dull-hearted: now he might sense those feelings welling up uncontrollably. He would see his father's steeple-less church, and beyond a curtain of elms the Digweeds' rented Tudor manor. Then he would come to downhill pasture and he might be running so hard he could barely see. An observer might find him rather absurd, as a small boy in an elaborate uniform running down a flinty land with fists in the air. But Frank had a sense of purpose: he was coming home. He could talk with his father before returning to the red gundecks of King George's Navy, and with the affectionate greeting of a brother he might press his sisters to his heart. (7)

Honan does several things in this paragraph. He brings the environs of the Austen house alive with sensory detail. He then adds to those the details that spring up from his informed imagination like the coachman complaining about having the varnish scratched off or the small running boy "with his fists in the air." He sprinkles this imaginative account with factual detail: The inn where Jane and Cassandra often collected their mail (bringing to mind their well-known correspondence), the steepleless church of Reverend George Austen, Jane's father, or the name of their neighbours, the Digweeds. We see the country side on a spring day through Frank's eyes or what Honan researched and imagined Frank to have seen, together with details of Frank's own account. All this merges to recreate an atmosphere.

This is a method used often in the dramatized documentaries of our day. Honan works like a director who is in control of the information he wants to present and knows exactly the sense he wants to convey. He creates the scene in his imagination blending fact and fiction even referring to an "observer" who watches the scene. The "observer" is both himself, the biographer, and us, the readers – allowed to be our own Boswell so to speak and "be there" as Frank Austen runs home. This fictionalization or dramatization is what produces the liveliness of Honan's narrative and creates a sense of immediacy despite the objectivity imposed by a temporal distance of almost two centuries. Honan puts the social, political, cultural, familial, physical and topographical together as if he were putting together the pieces of a jigsaw, which would incidentally be quite an appropriate description his narrative strategy.

The paragraph quoted above is the last one of "Prelude: Frank Austen's Ride Home." Apart from the sensory images and the progression towards Austen's home, this paragraph also makes linguistic reverberations. The contemporary English of the paragraph gently reverts back to the eighteenth century and ends in an expression Jane Austen herself uses in her novels: Frank might "with the affectionate greeting of a brother [...] press his sisters to his heart" (7). This gentle retreat to Austen's language is an excellent transition to the next chapter which starts the chronological telling of Austen's life.

Honan's "jigsaw method" extends over the entire life narrative. The first chapter of Part I does not abruptly turn to the year of Austen's birth or, as many other biographies do, reach immediately back to the story of Austen's ancestors in Kent. It follows from where the "Prelude" leaves off. Frank comes home and is greeted warmly by his family. There is a brief look at who is who in the house and where the house is situated. Integrated into our introduction to the family is its history. The transitions are smooth: Honan says that "Jane herself was enthralled by her father's story and perhaps their name was respectably old in Kentish and Sussex families" (12). This sentence works as a transition to the family history.

Honan tries to bring the sense of the past into the present in every way he can. He points to places, especially buildings that survive without much alteration since Austen's day: "The Red House still stands on the airy, hilly High Street to remind us of Jane Austen's family" (13). Although one knows that historically a certain person or family lived at a certain place, at a certain time, it is still difficult to grasp the reality of their lives after so many years. Honan knows this human weakness and tries to include as many concrete traces of life as possible to build a bridge between then and now.

The part on Austen's childhood, which can be thought of as an introductory section of the biography, is full of physical descriptions of the characters. In these early chapters, not only the landscape but also people's profiles take shape. Mrs Austen was "short, fragile, pretty and disinclined to marry" (15) when she was young, she had "fine cut features, large grey eyes, and, good eyebrows" (15); "Mr Austen's eyes were not large, but of a particular and bright hazel" (12). Particularly in these childhood chapters Honan draws a solid, material world. He documents and numbers almost every stone which enhances our sense of a thoroughly researched biography. Among these well-created scenes of lived life, Jane Austen starts moving to the foreground. First she and her sister "Cassy" are shown as the only girls among eight siblings. Their existence is created through the accounts of others:

> Soon they walked hand in hand, and Mr Austen often thought of them as one. His fine featured face and neat attire confronted them when he called out, with delight, to 'the girls'. Anna Lefroy later recalled the oddity of his referring to *grown* daughters as 'girls' in such pleasant tones. 'Where are the girls?' he would cry. 'Are the girls gone out?' They dressed alike and lived in unison: 'I remember too their bonnets,' says Anna, 'because though perfectly alike in colour, shape and material, it made it a pleasure to guess, & I believe I always guessed right, which bonnet [and girl belonged] to each other. (23)

The time the sisters spend at the Abbey School at Reading is the point in the narrative where Honan starts to show Austen's intellectual formation. He gives a list of the books she read. He bases this knowledge on sound evidence: Some of the books are alluded to in her *Juvenilia*, some are given to her as birthday presents and some are compulsory reading at schools like Abbey. Her reading is associated with her writing, and through these associations Honan presents her works: "Hence there is a tendency in young Jane Austen to find the world by racing through bad novels to measure their absurdity against norms of her own close, sanely affectionate family" (35): A statement which easily brings Catherine Morland of *Northanger Abbey* to mind. Alongside her reading, people surrounding Austen shaped the way she looked at the world. None was more influential for a young girl, it seems, than the delightful Eliza de Feuillide, Austen's cousin on her father's side. Her background is told in the novel-like narrative that it deserves, and her influence on *Mansfield Park* is subtly hinted at. Starting with the popular, outgoing Eliza, Honan passes onto a discussion of Austen's shyness: "She shone in no crowd and needed the intimacy of 'family' to feel like herself" (63). Her moodiness, her introvert nature – not seen substantially in more idealizing biographies – are presented by the accounts of friends and family like Anna Lefroy and Eliza Austen. Her shyness is then connected to her talents of observation.

Starting from Austen's early days Honan never lets the political realities of the times out of sight: If the French War or the Revolution fired Austen's imagination in some way, the parlour of the Austen house was especially beneficial for the flowering of her genius. In this respect, Honan's integration of life inside and outside of Austen's home becomes a powerful tool to depict that milieu which nurtured her early literary output up until the Bath years.

Honan also devotes substantial amount of space to his discussion of love and affection in Austen's life. In a chapter entitled simply "Love," he talks about her love for her sister, brothers and also about romantic love and Austen's personal experience of it. He colours this subject with Austen's special fondness for love songs and her love of music in general. Austen's music notebooks and scores survive. Honan gives examples from these, telling us what she liked, when she played, how she copied the scores in her neat hand, thus greatly adding to the sense of lived life (99). Her fondness for love songs is paralleled with her belief in love: "Love songs relieved and delighted her, even soppy ones. She believed in love, and used merciless realism against a world that threatened it, though she knew that love is comic itself" (99).

The world in which Austen circulated as a young woman is described with its contrasting sides, both dreamy and real. Honan creates the exciting atmosphere of young people anticipating a ball, then makes the following remark: "There *was* a vicious new pace in 'matrimonial affairs' in Hampshire these days: music, dancing and dress were more competitively used as men became fewer in wartime" (103). He spares more than enough pages for her flirtation with Tom Lefroy, proving with his jigsaw method that she was indeed in love – a question often asked by people interested in Austen's life and works. Seemingly advocating Elizabeth Jenkins's[3] idea that it would be impossible for her to depict love as she did if she had not fallen in love herself, Honan handles the issue with typical self-confidence and his account sounds convincing.

Bath, Austen's residence after Steventon, is also described in the visually strong Honan style. Austen goes to Bath to look for a house:

> To go about honey-coloured streets looking over railings into gray and empty area-ways, following an uncle's clumping stick to yet another terrace and then to wonder about the sizes of rooms, about furniture and about where one might sleep, dine and converse can be for a while a pleasing pursuit" (179).

A town of beautiful, elegant architecture and an exciting social life; a town Austen disliked. "[...] but much was lacking, and much, much was wrong no matter how well she loved her parents. They did not

[3] Another Austen biographer; she wrote *Jane Austen*.

transform Bath any more than grass beyond Sydney Place compensated for her Steventon" (183), says Honan. The discomfort of Bath and its negative effect on Austen's creativity are in the same chapter with the only known marriage proposal she receives. This is an interesting choice. By doing so, Honan manages to put in perspective why Austen first accepts then declines the proposal.

He first briefly gives the history of the Bigg-Wither family. Austen is a friend of the daughters of Lovelace Bigg-Wither, Catherine and Alethea. They have a brother, Harris. After the Austens move to Bath, Jane and Cassandra receive an invitation from these two young ladies. Honan draws attention to how much pleasure this invitation must have given to Jane since she was looking forward to a place "linked to the delightful days of her girlhood" (188). She visits the house where she feels quite at home, away from the noise of Bath, the city of "white glare" (189). A week after their arrival the young master of the house proposes to Jane Austen. There are no accounts of Harris Bigg-Wither directly by Austen. Honan fills this gap with descriptions by Caroline Austen (her niece) and Reginald Bigg-Wither. He is reported to be awkward, uncouth, quick tempered and rude – and he stutters. "At twenty one," Honan writes, "he was very probably a silent admirer. Jane, who was six years older than Harris, at least half-pitied him as she was much more alert, worldly, sensible and controlled [...]" (191).

Honan aptly compares the beautiful and vast grounds of Harris's home with the grounds Austen imagined for Darcy's Pemberley in *Pride and Prejudice*. This compassion is appropriate because "[...] for six days with Catherine and Alethea she had known delights of old wainscoated chambers, and of beautiful historical settings" (192). Given their family circumstances and that "marriage is the greatest felicity on earth, as mother believed [...] to have said no to Harris Wither would have been patently foolish and very nearly selfish" (193).

Austen thinks about her decision through the night. Her thoughts during that night, the pros and cons she probably went through in her mind are presented in a two-pages long paragraph. It is not a stream--

of-consciousness narration, but gives us the impression that we are overhearing Austen's inner debate. Again there is no written record by Austen herself about that night.[4] The closest we can get to her is through Fanny Lefroy, "who heard of this night from Anna Lefroy whose mother actually talked to Jane Austen some twelve hours after Harris Wither's proposal" (194). Too far for comfort – but biographers must make the best of what they have. Austen, after the night of reflection, gets a "revulsion of feeling" according to this account and reverses her decision in the morning. Honan is aware of the circuitous nature of the evidence and follows it with a summary of how the episode is handled in family letters and previous popular biographies of Austen, such as those by Lord David Cecil and Elizabeth Jenkins. Honan is also careful to narrate the aftermath of the refusal and the different reactions – positive or otherwise – of the people around Austen. All in all, this seems to be the most comprehensive treatment of the episode among Austen biographies and a depiction which communicates the sense of ambiguity, confusion, blame and later relief which Austen must have felt.

Honan's *Jane Austen* is not strictly a critical biography. The creation of the novels are chronologically placed at their right places within the narrative, then they are followed by two to three page "readings" which attempt to put the works in perspective within the artistic development of the author. But we must note a weakness in these readings. Honan draws the parallels between real life and characters and events in the novels too emphatically. One should be more wary when speaking of direct influences in the case of an author of Austen's sophistication. Concerning Austen's cousin Eliza, Honan says,

---

[4] Jane Austen's sister Cassandra burnt all her letters that she considered to be too private.

> Yet without Eliza *Northanger Abbey* might be different. Its heroine is amusing partly because of its detached, alert narrator. Eliza with amoral daring and spirit had cut through English society and in her letters had offered a detached, foreign and amused view of the present so that her example helped Jane Austen to make a fresh view of society and an affectionate view of the Gothic craze. (138)

This is giving Austen's own artistic sensibilities and judgment too little credit, and is combined with a wish to make use of every source available in every possible connection. In the discussion of *Sense and Sensibility* Honan writes, "Fanny's 'Sense' in contrast with Anna's 'madness' and impulsive rash independence offered traits of her own Elinor and Marianne" (274-75).

Nevertheless, the critical sections have insightful statements both about the author and the novels. Statements like "She had found that realism of a heroine's viewpoint depends on an illusion of the narrator's separate integrity" (145) or "the sisters are symbiotic; as Elinor looks after Marianne so Marianne gives her something to be moral and sensible about" make these sections interesting to read. Also Honan is careful enough to inform the reader of a recent correction concerning *Mansfield Park*. For the longest time, critics read an Austen letter quite wrongly because of the faulty punctuation and capitalization in an edition of her letters. In the printed version of the letter Austen appears to say that *Mansfield Park* is about ordination. Several articles were written on that false premise. What Austen actually writes in her letter is that she is going to change the subject she has been writing about; she would no longer write about her novel *Mansfield Park* but about a totally different topic: ordination at her brother James's rectory.

Honan also writes about *Sanditon*, Austen's unfinished last novel, in some detail. In his usual manner he passes on from the last written joke in *Sanditon* to Jane's last illness. As almost all biographers do before him, he relies heavily on Austen's last letters in this section of the book. Characteristically, he describes the view from her sickroom's window at Winchester. As Austen approaches her end Honan also brings us up to date about her brothers. In the final scene he talks about the time when Cassandra sits by her sister's side on 15th July 1817, and then he talks about other matters, delaying the moment of her death which took place three days later on the 18th. In between, he talks of her closeness to Cassandra and the small inheritance she leaves her, oddly juxtaposed with an overview of her literary legacy. Then comes the moment of death, told in the standard version with no addition of new detail.

The narrative ends with another ride, Cassandra coming home after her beloved sister's funeral in Winchester. This ride gives the text a circularity, creating a sense of closure:

> Travelling east to her home, Cassandra went back along a chalk road. In Hampshire in July the lark sings day and night, and in towns the fern-owl begins chattering after dusk. Farmers cut their hedges and spread the hay. The bloom of the lime hangs in yellow tassels, and young swallows dart and sparkle in fields. Roses and irises and honeysuckles all make a show. (408)

The narrative of Austen's life beginning with a brother and ending with a sister symbolizes how her life was encircled by her family. Honan's conclusion reaffirms what her nephew Edward Austen's implied after Jane Austen's death, that "her family were enormously more important to her than the world" (183).

If the biographies discussed in previous chapters can be called "people oriented" in terms of background, Honan's *Jane Austen, Her Life* can be called a "place/space oriented" biography. After reading the work, one has a strong sense of place, and in certain instances, of landscape. This provides some portion of the sense of vividness, immediacy, or lived life which Honan gets across to the reader. His jigsaw method is especially successful in creating this solid background.

However, this method is not without certain drawbacks. It is prone to exaggeration and confusion of fact and fiction. While many of the opinions in the book are directly quoted with appropriate documentation some are more impressionistic, and they combine several sources: "Mr Austen was concerned with advancing his four healthy sons and yet he realized that his wife was no longer young. It pleased him no doubt to find her 'nimble and active' as she awaited the birth of a seventh baby in November" (20). How does Honan know this? The statement sounds speculative, even presumptuous; the narrative voice almost knows too much and fails to create the intimacy it sets out to do. How much of what is written in that paragraph is from a source and how much is Honan's interpretation? It is difficult to tell. This ambiguity is quite disturbing for readers who want to know where they stand in relation to fact and fiction in a biography. Such ambiguous writing also results in occasional inconsistencies. About the adoption of Austen's brother Edward by rich relatives, Honan first says that "his parents planned to give him away" (24). Then, a paragraph later, he says, "Mr Austen was quick to oblige a relative, but he hesitated to give away a son of fifteen or sixteen" (25). Which of these statements is true? The style prevents even an educated guess.

This ambiguity is sometimes covered over by the narrative voice. It speaks with a self-assurance, a boldness which makes the reader take certain statements at face value as in "She believed in love" (99). The blending of source material and interpretation creates a very intimate voice, however Honan himself is strangely absent from his text. The same element which creates the intimacy of tone keeps the biographer at bay.

Almost all biographers who are historically distant from their subjects prepare a long list of acknowledgments for their biographies. Neither Honan's *Jane Austen, Her Life* nor Andrew Motion's *Keats* is an exception. The list includes names of distant relatives, owners of private collections of letters, memoirs and other documents, librarians, curators of museums, personnel in records offices, previous biographers "who kindly lent their assistance," friends, colleagues, co-workers, assistants, secretaries who offered their services in proof-reading or typing. "Look," the biographer seems to say, "how much approval and assistance I have – I don't know my subject personally, and I do not know anyone who knew my subject, but I have the next best thing. I have all the resources and professional guidance available to a contemporary biographer": Acknowledgments are a sort of recommendation letter addressed to the reader.

* * *

Andrew Motion's *Keats* has two such acknowledgments, one for illustrations and another for the text. At first glance, they seem to be standard lists of names and mainly, they are. However, the acknowledgment for the text has an important and telling detail: a tribute to "the three biographies of Keats in the 1960s" (xv). Motion, the winner of the first Whitbread Award for Biography in 1971 with his *Philip Larkin: A Writer's Life* is himself a poet[5] and picks a popular nineteenth century poet as his subject. He states that he has written his version as if in dialogue with these three earlier biographies: "In what follows, I have quoted from them, agreed with them, and disagreed with them, in much the same way I would want to treat people who had known Keats personally" (xv). Here he establishes himself in the biographical tradition and at the same time underlines his difference as a biographer historically removed from his subject. In the absence of relatives and/or friends to interview, he turns to previous research, interpretation and insight. Biography, in this sense, becomes self-referential. In Motion's case, the biographer again turns into a surrogate who knows the subject with some intimacy – next best thing to one who personally knew the subject.

[5] Motion's ten years as Poet Laureate of United Kingdom ended in 2009.

The book consists of fifty-four chapters. In contrast to the two biographies written by Holroyd and Honan in the second half of the twentieth century, the chapters have neither titles nor epigraphs. Yet like the Holroyd and Honan biographies, it does have an introduction. Motion starts by stating, in a Johnsonian manner, the universal appeal of Keats's life. It has something to offer to readers in any walk of life: "Readers have made him a byword for poetic identity. At once pathetic and sublime, his story distills familiar human fears, and realizes the most noble ideas. Its fascination is endless; its power to move and inspire is inexhaustible" (xix).

Keats is presented here as an ideal subject for biography. His sublimity inspires and his pathetic side is capable of arising empathy in any reader. The "human fears" we find in his life are points of connection between him and the reader. The influence of his life spills over from the pages of the biography "to move and inspire," which means that it will translate into other lives – a primary justification for life writing.

The story of Keats's life can do just that if its "reality" can be fully communicated. But is not this easy to do for a conscientious biographer? According to Motion it is not. Keats's "posthumous existence" stands between him and his readers. Motion says that "the translation of his life into a legend has distorted or denied important aspects of his achievement" (xix). Here we can find the pointers to a mission for the biographer. The biographer may be the person who re-evaluates this "posthumous existence," clears away the mists of legend, and enables the reader to see Keats in a new light as he really was. Motion's task is especially difficult. The idealization of Keats is a process which started two hundred years ago, largely due to the writings of P. B. Shelley and Leigh Hunt. Keats's reputation also

> depended greatly on the approval of a female audience. But just as Victorian readings of his poetry denied its political charge, so they also made its pagan sensuality conform to a

> more sedate aesthetic. The effect was paradoxically to emphasise his 'effeminacy', making him seem especially sympathetic to the very readers he had gone out of his way to repudiate. The biographies written by Amy Lowell, Blanche Williams and Dorothy Hewlett show the tendency persisting in more recent times. (605)

Therefore, the biographer has to fight against a false image long petrified in the minds of the reading public.

The first full length biography of Keats, written by Richard Monckton Milnes in 1848, tried to sift through the idealization but was not "adequately equipped" according to Motion. This early biographer was weighed down by Victorian reticence and morality, he "played down the troublesome political dimension" and "radicalism" in his poetry" (xx). Motion mentions five biographies which followed Milnes's and shows in what way they promoted the image of the "escapist and effete" artist, "softening the outline of his ambition" (xxi). In the 1950s Keats's papers and letters came to light and were annotated. However, the biographies that came out after the publication of new material enhanced the previous image. They still implied that Keats lived in an aesthete's vacuum. Motion describes how such interpretations came about and uses the introduction as a platform to describe what he will work against. He thus lays down the foundation for his own ideas about Keats. The cornerstone of this foundation will be Keats's radicalism – something that has been ignored or taken lightly all along: "It is to show that his efforts to crystallise moments of 'truth' combine a political purpose with a poetic ambition, a social search with an aesthetic ideal" (xxv). Thus creating a niche for himself in and against the biographical tradition surrounding Keats, he declares his justification for yet another Keats biography:

> There is good reason to believe that the lives of all-important writers need to be reconsidered at regular intervals, no matter how familiar they might be. While the wind of history blows,

> their stories revolve and alter, offering new attractions and sometimes new difficulties to each successive generation. This might be reason enough for wanting to add another *Life* of Keats to those that already exist, even supporting that his radicalism had already been adequately described. As it is, the justification is more substantial. The Keats that has come down to us is finely figured, yet incomplete. (xxv)

Motion is there to complete what is left incomplete and he opens the biography at a time close to Keats's death – imbuing the text with the idea of death just like Keats's own life was imbued with it:

> In September 1820, five months before his death, Keats sailed to Italy with his friend Joseph Severn. Their journey along the south coast of England was disrupted by a series of terrible storms and exasperating calms. Often their boat was driven backwards the way it had come. Occasionally the captain allowed his passengers ashore while he waited for a favourable wind. During one of these delays, they explored 'the splendid caverns and grottos' around Lulworth Cove, in Dorset. Keats told Severn it was 'a part [of England] he already knew', but did not say precisely how or why. His reticence was characteristic. Throughout his life he made very few remarks about his early days, and none about his distant ancestors. (3)

If the first image that is associated with Keats is death, the second image is his reticence, and how even his closest friends did not really know about his early life. The reticent young man is in contrast to the idea of the babbling, overly sentimental Romantic. "The splendid caves and grottos around Lulworth Cave in Dorset" that are mentioned in this first paragraph also allude obliquely to Keats's reticence and his premature death – the still unexplored corners of the poet's creative mind, a potent image to start a biography.

Just as he announces in the acknowledgments, Motion keeps up a constant dialogue with other biographies throughout the work. This adds a meta-biographical tinge to the narrative. The reader is often reminded that this biography is an interpretation of Keats's life and is in no way "definitive" – maybe only restorative. He includes statements like "Over the years, biographers have struggled to fill in the details of his background" within his own narrative. By criticizing the reliability of one of the most substantial sources of Keats's early life, Richard Abbey, the guardian of the Keats children after the death of their parents, he points at the difficulties in evaluating sources – thereby drawing attention to the backstage mechanics of biography.

Keats's parental origins, it seems, were never clearly known to himself and to people around him. However, Keats could have learned more about them if he had wanted to according to Motion. His distant relatives are certainly within his reach at the time he lives in London. Masterfully, Motion links Keats's conscious choice of being somewhat indifferent to his family to what he was to become as a poet:

> Writing to his sister-in-law in 1818 he said awkwardly but proudly that his name had been 'Enchanted ... the Lord knows where,' and even the letters he sent to those he loved best were often signed simply 'Keats'. This signature encapsulated feelings which shaped his whole existence. Forgetting or concealing his origins, he longed to turn himself from a private citizen into a poetic landmark. (5)

In fact, the centripetal direction exemplified above can be felt in the entire narrative. Every detail is turned over to the service of Keat's poetry and his poetic identity. This a more concentrated centrality than what we have seen in both Holroyd's and Honan's biographies, coming closer to Boswell's *Life of Johnson* – one fundamental difference being that there is a greater amount of dialogue between the subject's creative output and his life story. For example, Motion believes that Thomas Keats, a boat owner in the transportation business, may be

Keats's father. The evidence on this issue is not very strong. However, Motion does not want to dismiss a possible connection that can be made between Keats's childhood and his later poetic inclinations. Reflections of a life near a river or the sea are immediately identified in Keats's poetry:

> This boat-owning Thomas Keats moved inland in 1770, perhaps elsewhere in Devon, *perhaps* to Berkshire. In any event, it is likely that memories of his previous life came with him, and *possible* that in due course these were passed on to Keats himself. His writing often uses images to do with sea. He describes himself as 'leap[ing] headlong into the sea' when he begins *Endymion*; he refers to 'dead-drifting' and to casting an anchor 'stiff'; and all manner of tides and currents run between his earliest 'Imitation of Spencer' and his epitaph: 'Here lies one whose name is writ in water'. (5; emphases mine)

Motion revises the popular images of some of the figures in Keats's life as well. His mother Frances Jennings had been identified as "a flirt" by the spiteful family "friend" Richard Abbey (8). But turning to sources less likely to be biased against her, Motion gives a more "sensible" image. As a result, she emerges as a strong character:

> [...] George Keats insisted that 'She was a most excellent and affectionate parent and as I thought a woman of uncommon talent.' The reports make Frances less like the flirt that Abbey described, and more like an obviously pretty, capable and vivacious woman, someone who was naturally strong-willed, and who throughout her childhood had been encouraged to think and act for herself. She was clearly frustrated by the lack of opportunities that life offered so long as she remained single. (9)

The marriage of Keats's parents is sometimes called "a hasty affair," but Motion dismisses the idea with "there is no corroborating evidence for this" (9). Evidence is what Motion is very particular about; all statements coming from direct sources are marked and shown in the notes. This creates a clean-cut relationship between what is fact and what is Motion's interpretation.

Political history in particular marks the background of Motion's biography. The effects of the political and, consequently, the social climate of the age on Keats's life are the backbone of Motion's biographical idea. He does not present history in a novelistic manner as Honan does. The voice is matter-of-fact and detached:

> As the Industrial Revolution picked up speed in the mid-eighteenth century, new kinds of economic activity had proliferated, stimulated by advances in iron production, in clay manufacture, in cotton spinning, in steam power, in road and water communication. The population increased rapidly; markets boomed [...]. (11)

This neutrality is not only apparent in sections where Motion talks of history, but also in literary interpretation. The world of writing and publishing is also depicted in detail. Motion believes that Keats's school life was a formative influence on his creativity. When there is eyewitness information on any place, Motion uses that instead of rewording it. The description of the school grounds is a good example of this:

> Beyond it stretched a garden, part of which was given over to small plots to be cultivated by the pupils themselves. Clarke's [the headmaster] son described the setting as rural paradise: 'a magnificent old morello cherry tree' grew against the house 'well exposed to the sun'; beyond the garden lay 'a sweep of grass, in the centre of which was a pond sometimes dignified as a lake' where the boys learned to swim; [...] be-

> yond the pond was an iron railing across which the 'song of nightingales' drifted from nearby woods; and built against this railing was 'a rustic arbour' where, towards the end of his time at the school, Keats stands reading Spencer's *The Faerie Queene*. (24)

Notice again how the description gravitates towards Keats's poetry, particularly to "Ode to a Nightingale."

Motion stays away from speculation when no evidence can be found. He does not try to fill in the gaps with whatever evidence he can find about other people in his life or the neighbours as Honan is sometimes prone to do. For example, there is practically no recorded evidence about the days Keats spent as an apprentice to Thomas Hammond. Motion writes: "Little evidence survives about his daily doings with Keats and only a few anecdotes give them any vivid colouring," and later he adds openly, "such details hardly shed enough life to illuminate a day, let alone five years" (50). Motion's attitude is important in that he does not suffer from the twentieth century biographer's disease of trying to explain everything. Although he does try to put many aspects of Keats's life into perspective, and most importantly to expand our understanding of his poetry, he leaves room for the inexplicable.

> He was extraordinarily young when he produced his greatest poetry. Although never prodigious in the sense that Mozart was prodigious, and although his friends recognized this by stressing what Hunt called his 'great promise' rather than his maturity, the fact remains that he was only twenty-three years old when he wrote 'The Eve of St. Agnes', the six odes, 'Lamia' and the two 'Hyperion's. Accounts of his reading, his friendships, his psychological imperatives, his poetic 'axioms', his politics, and his context can never completely explain this marvellous achievement. The story of his life must also allow for other things – things which have become em-

> barrassing or doubtful for many critics in the late twentieth century, but which are still as they always were actual and undeniable: inspiration, accident, genius. (xxv)

The time of apprenticeship with Hammond is also the beginning of Keats's life as a poet. Starting with the first example of his poetry, and the "Epistle to Charles Cowden Clark" dating from September 1816, Motion quotes extensively from poems, comments on them in detail and connects them tightly to the life story. The single most remarkable achievement of this biography is its mastery in blending Keats's daily life with his intellectual, emotional, and artistic development. In this respect, *Keats* is a true literary biography, where life sheds light on works and works shed light on life. It is so well balanced that one does not overwhelm the other.

Being a poet himself, Motion is in his element while criticizing Keats's poems. The criticism is done in an informed, unexaggerated, unsentimental tone, praising where praise is due and making unflattering remarks when he must; "saying this makes the poems sound better then they are", he says at one point – distancing himself from his previous descriptions of "sweet solutions" and "fine excess" (71). This tone greatly enhances the biography's overall air of reliability and objectivity. As Motion traces Keats's poems he also traces books he reads. So, we have an idea of what the poet was reading as he wrote his poems. The readings and poems are expected to form certain connections in the reader's mind – and Motion often points those out himself. Keats was reading Wordsworth as he wrote "O Solitude!" Such connections enrich the biography no doubt; however, they also make it a biography for the well-read. Yet, this may be unavoidable since the genre discussed is poetry, and Motion sets out to write a "literary biography."

Keats's relations with women in general and with his friend's sister Fanny Brawne in particular are also related to his poetry. His desire for women is sometimes expressed in an embarrassed, disguised way in his poems. Concerning his relationship with Fanny Brawne too, there are all sorts of conflicts. Motion again and again emphasizes Keats's contradictory feelings about marriage; he quotes directly from his letters on this topic: "I have spoken to you against Marriage, but it was general – the Prospect in those matters has been so blank, that I have not been unwilling to die [...]" (283).

Keats is anxious about whether he can support a family on his writing, the complications a wife and child may bring to his life as a poet, the influence of marriage on the protection of the creative self. He is in a way afraid of Fanny, translated in the following lines:

> She stings me through! –
> Even as the worm doth feed upon the nut
> So she, a scorpion, preys upon my brain!
> I feel her gnawing here! (*Otho the Great* 5.5; qtd. in
> Motion 421)

On the other hand, when he discovers that he is slowly dying in the famous scene where he coughs and observes his own blood, his thoughts immediately turn to Fanny. His friend Brown relates:

> On entering the cold sheets, before his head was on the pillow, he slightly coughed, and I heard him say, "That is blood from my mouth." I went towards him; he was examining a single drop of blood upon the sheet. "Bring me the candle, Brown; and let me see this blood." After regarding it steadfastly, he looked up in my face, with a calmness of countenance that I can never forget, and said, "I know the colour of that blood; – it is arterial blood; – I cannot be deceived in that colour; – the drop of blood is my death warrant; – I must die". (Qtd. in Motion 496)

"All he could think about was Fanny, and 'the love which has so long been my pleasure and torment,'" writes Motion (496). He does not try to hide the contradictions and "torment" involved in Keats's love for Fanny. On the contrary, he shows the dynamism and depth this love brings to his art.

The penultimate chapter of the book centres inevitably on Keats's final days. Motion discusses Keats's early irritability and later calmness during that time. Keats talks about his funeral arrangements with his friend Severn. He wants Severn to go look at the Protestant cemetery outside Rome where he will be buried. Pleased with Severn's account of sheep and goats grazing at the graveyard, Keats says, "The spring was always enchantment to me [...] perhaps the only happiness I had in the world – has been the silent growth of flowers" (564). Such quotations add to the sadness of the final days of someone so young and so talented. As in most biographies, the final scene is told through the account of the person nearby. Perhaps the most affecting aspect of this scene is the directness of its presentation and Motion's simple words following the results of the autopsy: "Keats's lungs were almost completely destroyed; Clark pronounced it the worst case of consumption he had ever seen. He could not imagine how Keats had lived for so long. Keats was twenty-five years and four months old" (567).

Motion follows Keats's friends after his death in the second half of the penultimate chapter. Fanny Brawne's reaction, other people's reaction to her mourning, and their misunderstanding of her attitude towards Keats are discussed in some detail. From there on Motion follows the birth of Keats's legend, "the distortions by Shelley" and "the dwarfing by Byron" end this chapter. However, the final chapter is spent on the attempts at restoring Keats's reputation, his "robustness" (575).

Motion chooses the question "How long is this posthumous life of mine to last?" for his last paragraph. This is a question Keats asked his friend Clark in Rome (577). Motion answers it with the fact that Keats has been made immortal through his readers. And he leaves the final words to Keats's friend Woodhouse, the editor of a collection of Keats's poems:

> His sentences do not have the surge of a resounding conclusion. Rather, they make an appropriately 'awkward bow'. They insist that Keats deserves eternal fame because the astoundingly rich world of his invention contained 'a very great deal of reality'. 'There must be'. Woodhouse wrote, 'many allusions to particular Circumstances, in his poems: which would add to their beauty & Interest, if properly understood. – To arrest some few of those circumstances, & bring them to view in connexion with the poetic notice of them, is one of the objects of this collection'. (578)

Motion chooses this quotation to end his narrative because it summarizes what he himself aims at in *Keats*. And he certainly achieves this aim: The "circumstances" of Keats's life lend a context of reality to the poems and enhance their aesthetic value while the poems render life with aesthetic value, like "the silent growth of flowers."

Andrew Motion's *Keats* satisfies all requirements of contemporary biography: it is well researched, it makes use of primary material in a thorough and balanced way, it does highlight new and previously untouched aspects of the subject's life. The narrative voice is objective and the style is closer to social history than to the novel. This neutrality creates a sense of unmediated flow of information. All documents are well-integrated; one does not outweigh any other. Social, political, and private histories are masterfully blended with one another. However – or maybe as a consequence – Motion is not able to create a sense of lived life or immediacy which in one way or another was present in the previously discussed biographies. This may lead one to conclude that it is actually the idiosyncrasies of the biographies – the ways in which the biographers tell their stories – that give the books a sense of lived life. The only idiosyncrasy of Motion's *Keats* is that it has none. This does not mean that Motion's book is an inconsequential biography, on the contrary, it is an example that gives us a chance to observe what happens when theoretical ideals of biography are perfectly met.

Afterword

> A study of biographies by the dozen, though it often leaves one pretty much in the dark as to the people biographised, ought perhaps to give some view as to the art of biography.
>
> Leslie Stephen, *"National Biography"*

The half a dozen biographies discussed in this book all point to a "fundamental paradox" innate in biography as a genre: A biography "can gain completeness only by selectivity" (Nadel 207). The biographer aims to reconstruct a life in such a way that it not only corresponds to the factual realities of the subject's life but also conveys a vivid, rounded, immediate sense of "lived life." The first is given, concrete; the second is created. This creation is done through language and narration, which together give the "telling of a life" a coherent form, a completeness which life itself is said to lack. After all, a life cannot be "told/written," it can only be lived; it is the story of a life that can be told/written. So, is completeness desirable and necessary in biographical narrative? Until the end of the twentieth century the answer to this question would be, more often than not, a "yes". Biographies that narrated the subject's story "from cradle to grave" or "from womb to tomb" were the norm. The foremost attraction of such a narrative with a beginning, a middle, and an end is the simple pleasure of following the entire life-story of an individual where pieces slowly fit together to form the finished and finally revealed picture. This sense of completeness emphasizes the narrative's exemplary and consequently moral implications, it illuminates the particular historical moment that belongs to the subject, and it "suggests to the attentive reader that within his own fragmented existence, there is a teleological unity" (Nadel 208). From Johnson to Boswell, from Strachey to Motion, we can see the biographies carry these functions of "completeness" in different degrees.

The teleological unity is an illusion created through various narrative strategies. No matter how strong a sense of completeness a biography exudes, no biographer does or can write under the pretence that a biography is actually a complete life story. As biographer and theoretician Leon Edel says in "The Poetics of Biography," a good biography presents "the complexities of being without pretending that life's riddles have been answered" (42). In this respect, biography is a highly self-conscious genre – always aware that "what it is" is formed by "how it is."

Each narrative strategy is a choice; however, no choice in biography can be made entirely freely. Each has to be defined by historical circumstances and the availability of sources. What significantly marks Johnson's *Life of Savage* and Boswell's *Life of Johnson* is the biographers' personal acquaintance with their respective subjects. Both narratives follow their subjects from birth to death. Obviously, they are not witnesses to their subjects' lives in their entirety, but what they do not personally know – which is quite a lot in both cases – they fill in with other personal accounts, memoirs, diaries, letters, research and educated guesses. What is remarkable is that, although personal acquaintance gives them an immense opportunity to create an intimate narrative, both seem to be running away from something: A suspicion that they will not or cannot be objective precisely because of the acquaintance.

Johnson tries to surmount the problem of objectivity by assuming a seemingly impersonal, omniscient, god-like narrative voice. Boswell, to the contrary, floods the narrative with his own voice repeating over and over again that he is objective. They also differ in the way they allow the subject's voice to be heard. Richard Savage is heard twice, through a speech he made in a courtroom, and through a few letters from prison. Boswell turns the narrative over to Johnson's authentic voice whenever possible. The concept that governs Johnson's *Life of Savage* is advocacy. He designs his biography in such a way that Savage emerges as a victim in need of a firm, articulate defender and as an invaluable moral example for the reading public. The entire narrative is geared towards this concept of protesting Savage's wrongs, at the same time making those wrongs into universals that the reader can identify with. The dominant concept in Boswell's *Life of Johnson*, on the other hand, is preservation. Boswell often uses the metaphor of embalming in the text. His narrative is geared towards arresting instances of his subject's life in time and recording them for posterity: We may add to that Boswell's own urge for self-preservation as a friend of Johnson and as a writer.

Is the "distanceless" biographer able to escape the traps of hagiography? It seems not. Even the most accomplished biographers are not safe. Personal acquaintance seems to bring with it such complicated emotional entanglements that the biographer either feels the need to protect or the need to attack, as the case may be. However, the strength of the "distanceless biographer" is also undeniable. The vivid depiction of the subject is at the biographer's disposal, and this one advantage in the hands of a talented storyteller can minimize most flaws of craftsmanship.

The biographers who are roughly contemporaries of their subjects without forming an actual acquaintance with them can use their advantage by writing biographies against a historical, social or interpersonal backdrop. Both Lytton Strachey and Michael Holroyd do this in their biographies. Strachey's four short biographies in *Eminent Victorians* centre on the theme of Victorianism. This is Strachey's target. His is an anti-hagiography – a biography which debunks its subjects rather than exalts them. Each biography in this quartet is a testament to Strachey's strong negative feelings towards Victorianism, which, as he was born in 1880, is in fact an integral part of his upbringing. All his subjects except Dr Arnold were alive at the time of Strachey's birth, which means that people close to them were actually alive at the time of Strachey's composition. However, Strachey follows a different course than most biographers in his situation and chooses not to benefit from their knowledge. He prefers to use secondary material only.

This choice enables him to avoid any emotional closeness with his subjects. Strachey's aim necessitates a certain distance – but not too far. Consequently, his stance provides just the ideal blend of closeness and distance. His aversion towards Victorianism at a social level and towards strong ambition at a personal level seem to be the twin triggers in his attack.

Since the realm is biography, the weapon has to be a linguistic one: Strachey's is irony. He picks and chooses incidents, evidence, even letters and diary entries in such a way that they converge around only what he would like to present about his subject. In this sense, the wholeness of each of these four short pieces is unique. They do not give a complete picture of their subjects through the presentation of their diversity in all aspects of life, but a complete picture of one strong human trait that has put its stamp on almost all their actions. In this distorted completeness, subjects show the same traits of ambition even in their childhood. Strachey's iconoclastic attitude is made possible by the distance he puts between himself and his subjects, and this attitude is all the more noteworthy because it belongs to a Victorian-Edwardian. It carries the rebellious voice of a generation who has seen the First World War and the destructive role that the Victorian mindset has played in it.

The same distance handled differently makes Michael Holroyd's *Lytton Strachey: The New Biography* the important historical biography that it is. The completeness in this case comes from the detailed treatment of Strachey's entire life in all its aspects and the thorough use of personal material given to the biographer by the subject's brother and close friends. Holroyd uses the advantage of being a near contemporary of his subject by making personal contact with people who knew Strachey. This is the most remarkable aspect of the book. The actual narrative of the text is strictly connected to the preface. The reader first encounters figures like James Strachey, Frances Partridge or Harold Nicolson in this preface, sitting face to face with the living, breathing biographer. Because of this first encounter, the reader feels an enhanced sense of connectedness when the younger selves of those people appear in the narrative. Holroyd successfully projects the sense that although he does not know his subject personally, he has the advantage of the next best thing.

Since Holroyd is equipped with intimate primary material – letters from many of the members of the Bloomsbury group – he does not hesitate to let their multiple voices invade the narrative. His own narrative voice is quite detached, even cold as he tells Strachey's life story. However, in the sections describing and criticizing Strachey's literary output he becomes more visible and opinionated. Holroyd seems to think that two different realms of the narrative can be written in different voices. This choice on the biographer's part does not disrupt the narrative; on the contrary, Holroyd gives the impression that he is a biographer who knows when to give the reader assistance and when to step back. He also wants to emphasize Strachey's career as a biographer; therefore, it is natural that he appears to be more "present" when he wants to draw the reader's attention to Strachey's significance as a biographer.

Given the scope of the material at Holroyd's disposal, it was perhaps inevitable that he would write a biography which would involve interesting biographical information about people other than the subject. Strachey's correspondence with his friends from Cambridge and fellow Bloomsbury members forms a significant and colourful backdrop to Strachey's life story. In this sense, Holroyd's biography presents a panorama of an era and consequently a group picture of some of the most talented and prolific intellectuals of that era. This aspect brings Holroyd's biography close to Strachey's *Eminent Victorians*. On the one hand, the life of an individual is narrated, and on the other, a way of life and a state of mind are brought before the reader. Just as *Eminent Victorians* played a role in the comprehension and decoding of Victorianism, *Lytton Strachey* played a role in the late 1960s in the public advocacy of personal liberties, especially sexual ones. It also triggered an interest in the Bloomsbury group, both negative and positive. Since both biographies were written at times historically close to the eras they depicted, they had social and intellectual repercussions.

Biographers who write about subjects safely removed from their own times do not often cause a stir – unless of course they discover brand new material. Park Honan, like all biographers who choose a subject previously written about, states that his biography integrates new found family correspondence in its narrative, thereby making his version more complete than previous ones. Integration is a keyword for Honan's particular style of life-writing. He takes his subject's life-story as the skeleton and then fleshes it out with an immense variety of physical, social, and historical detail. He pays particular attention to creating a sense of place, in this case, of England during the Regency period. The integrated use of images rich in colour and sound with biographical information from written sources give a highly organic feel to this narrative. Honan prefers to combine information from different sources and express them in his own style rather than quoting from each separately, hence forming a unified narrative, which in turn constructs a strong sense of completeness. One of the effective methods late twentieth-century biographers use is to carry a novelistic and sometimes even a cinematographic approach into biography. This method greatly contributes to the historical atmosphere and Honan uses it extensively.

Keats's biographer Andrew Motion, like Honan, feels the need to write a few words to justify his biography. He states his dissatisfaction with the present sentimental, "Romantic" image of the poet created both by his contemporaries and his subsequent biographers, claiming that his biography will unearth Keats's energetic, politicized, "robust" character and put the poet in the right perspective. This does not preclude a "robust" narrative voice though. Motion is deliberately soft-spoken, keeping himself in the shadows as much as possible and leaving the stage to his subjects. The quietness of his tone makes it easy to forget the presence of the story-teller – something that is literally impossible to do in the other five biographies.

Motion's *Keats* is primarily a biography of a poet by a poet. The level of engagement with the subject's work in this biography puts the life-story in the service of the poetry. The dialogue between these two is the driving force of the narrative. Motion navigates through the possible difficulties of this dialogue without once falling into the trap of sentimentality. Motion avoids sentimentality not only in connection to Keats's poems but also at every other point in the text. The narrative voice is knowledgeable and objective, and provides illuminating insight.

This last biography forms an interesting contrast with the other five, and throws light on what might constitute a memorable biography. One would assume that the source of a biography's appeal would be the life-story of its subject. This assumption is of course correct, but only to a certain extent. The more biographies we read the more we realize that another aspect of biography has almost as strong a claim on its appeal as the life-story and that is the way the biographer tells the story. Motion's biography gathers all the "ideal" qualities of biography as stated above. However, it does not have any "quirkiness" or idiosyncrasy which makes it memorable. Dr Johnson's poorly disguised partiality; Boswell's delightful and sometimes infuriating ego; Strachey's irritated prejudice and ready-to-burst anger; Holroyd's freezing gaze and silent patience; Honan's insatiable need to "integrate, integrate, integrate" are what make their biographies some of the most remarkable examples of "the most delicate and humane of all the branches of writing" (Strachey, *Eminent Victorians* 10). Motion's biography has everything but "the Motion touch." In this case, the biographer's decision to be a barely felt presence in his narrative deprives the reader of witnessing one of the most intriguing and exciting relationships in writing.

* * *

At the end of the twentieth century, the idea to look at this relationship in a more detailed way opened a new direction for the genre. In

Keats's biography we find Andrew Motion reminding the reader that what he writes is only one version of Keats's possible life-narratives. He refers to other biographies of Keats, points out their flaws or strengths, and he once again reminds us that life-writing is a form with very close ties to fiction. As soon as the biographer picks and chooses, analyses, and rearranges – he becomes closer to a fiction writer. But will not the consciousness of this fact be also the death warrant of biography? Is not biography supposed to be a strict work of non-fiction to be acceptable? "Can the collection and ordering of data in a person's life ever give us complete knowledge of the truth, or must one recognize the fundamental inability of ever knowing the past exactly and therefore accept its fictions?" (Nadel 209). Some writers and scholars interested in the genre asked themselves these questions; the answers led to a deeper questioning of the intricacies of the biographer and subject dynamic. Since we have become aware of the impossibility of writing a biography proper, knowing what we know of the fictional quality of all writing, wouldn't it perhaps be enlightening to turn our gaze onto biography as a genre itself? Follow the development of a subject's image as depicted through biographies, look at how a life is fictionalized, see how each biographer creates his/her own subject out of the very same material, look at the ties that bind biographer to subject and take a step towards meta-biography?

Two works that can be called meta-biographies are Janet Malcolm's *The Silent Woman: Sylvia Plath and Ted Hughes* and Lucasta Miller's *The Brontë Myth: The Silent Woman* was first published in 1993 in *The New Yorker* and then turned into a book in 1994. Instead of writing a traditional biography, Malcolm chronicles, in a direct and captivating style, the ordeals biographers had to go through while trying to write Sylvia Plath's biography. As her other works also show, she "has been interested in transactions – between photographer and subject, psychoanalyst and patient, lawyer and witness." (Wood, n. pag.) So, the transaction between biographer and subject was particularly fascinating for her. She does not view the biographer and indeed the reader in a very positive light though:

> The biographer at work, indeed is like the professional burglar, breaking into the house, rifling through certain drawers that he has good reason to think contain the jewellery, and money, and triumphantly bearing his loot away. The voyeurism and busybodyism that impel writers and readers of biography alike are obscured by an apparatus of scholarship designed to give the enterprise an appearance of banklike blandness and solidity. The biographer is portrayed almost as a kind of benefactor. He is seen as sacrificing years of his life to his task, tirelessly sitting in archives and librar ies and patiently conducting interviews with witnesses. There is no length he will not go to, and the more his book reflects his industry the more the reader believes that he is having an elevating literary experience, rather than simply listening to backstairs gossip and reading other people's mail. The transgressive nature of biography is rarely acknowledged, but it is the only explanation of biography's status as a popular genre. The reader's amazing tolerance (which he would extend to no novel written half as badly as most biographies) makes sense only when seen as a kind of collusion between him and the biographer in an exciting forbidden undertak ing: tiptoeing down the corridor together to stand in front of the bedroom door and try to peep through the keyhole. (Malcolm 8)

Malcolm, a journalist first and foremost, and ever directed by the journalistic instinct, delves into what goes on behind-the-scenes during the preparation of a biography. Sylvia Plath's life which ended with suicide provides ample material for this kind of investigative work. She discusses several works on Plath such as Anne Stevenson's *Bitter Fame: A Life of Sylvia Plath*; Paul Alexander's *Rough Magic: A*

Biography of Sylvia Plath; Ronald Hayman's *The Death and Life of Sylvia Plath*; Linda Wagner-Martin's *Sylvia Plath: A Biography*; Edward Butscher's *Sylvia Plath: Method and Madness* and Jacqueline Rose's *The Haunting of Sylvia Plath*. Although Malcolm writes "scathing denunciation of the ethics of literary biography" (Showalter 3) she duplicates some of it practices such as sneaking around Ted Hughes's garden and publishing previously unpublished correspondence (Showalter 3). What the text overtly looks at and what Malcolm's subtext covertly suggests contributes to the compulsive readability of this work. Whenever the focus of discussion is Sylvia Plath biographies, inevitably, the formidable "Plath Estate" comes to the foreground. The Estate is, in effect, guarded by Ted Hughes (until his death in 1998) and his sister Olwyn Hughes. Against the tide, Malcolm emerges as a partial narrator siding with Ted and Olwyn Hughes. The story is full of excitement, adventure, burnt diaries, supressed and forbidden material, commissioned biographies, biographers on the verge of nervous breakdown, manipulation, distress and pain. It is a testament to emotional entanglement in biography writing. One emerges from the reading with a renewed and clearer than ever idea that there are as many "subjects" as there are biographers of that subject – there is absolutely no way to get at the "real" Sylvia Plath. She is all of what they say of her and none.

The new direction the genre took by looking at the afterlife of the subject through his/her biographies came into its own at the onset of the twenty-first century. In 2001, Lucasta Miller published *The Brontë Myth* which offered a sophisticated way of evaluating biography as an integral part of making cultural history. The book follows the legend created around Charlotte Brontë and, to a lesser degree, around her sisters Emily and Anne. While doing so, it enables us to follow the changes that biography as a genre has gone through over the years. "This book [...] is not so much a biography of the Brontë's but a book about biography, a metabiography. Occasionally, when focusing on the sentimental excesses of the Brontë cult, it may even read more like an anti-biography" (x), says Miller in her "Preface and Acknowledgements." To observe biographical writings from such a perspective highlights the historical and cultural components in the genre's make-up. The writers who are engaged with the genre are aware of its pitfalls, impossibilities as well as its cultural connections and possibilities. Now more than ever, this consciousness results in texts like Miller's which turn the critical gaze upon themselves – creating perhaps a more objective or scientific narrative tone:

> What I do not claim to be able to do – as too many biographers have claimed in the past – is to sweep away all previous 'fake' versions of the story and resurrect the 'true' Brontës in their place, as if the dead could be brought, definitively, back to life. Although recent scholars made enormous progress in reclaiming the factual circumstances and historical background of the Brontë experience, facts alone cannot provide the final word on a life, and there will always be a need for interpretation. [...]
>
> To acknowledge that all biographies have their own agenda and to reject the possibility of the definitive biography is not, however to deny that there are rights and wrongs when it comes to life-writing. (xi)

The self-awareness that Miller displays here is the new stamp on twenty-first century biographical writing and it is a step in the right direction, since it opens the genre to further explorations and possibilities.

Miller argues that Mrs Gaskell's biography, *The Life of Charlotte Brontë* (1857) was responsible for the Romantic image of the author. Subsequent life narratives, with the help of popular culture, perpetuated that image. As Miller moves among the myth making biographical texts, it is easy to see how she distrusts the genre because of its ever present inclination towards "fiction." However, this distrust does not prevent her from tracing her own version of the Brontë story, alongside her observations on the creation of the myth. Her version is a down-to-earth, persuasive version and her call "to turn the tables and put the writings first" (255), heartfelt and apt.

* * *

The first decade of the twenty-first century presented yet another alternative way to tell the life-story of a subject. This alternative particularly drew attention to biography's deep connection to history – but this time at a micro level. We should remember that in Ancient Greece and Rome, lives of leading public figures were inevitably included in histories, and at first life-writing was considered inseparable from history, which implicitly emphasized the genre's factual nature. Later many a biography was valued for the vivid historical backdrop it provided to a life, hence becoming primarily a historical source. However, biographers like James Shapiro and Charles Nicholl did not choose to write a sweeping life of their subject, but concentrated on a very specific period in his life.

James Shapiro in his 2005 biography, *A Year in the Life of William Shakespeare: 1599*, focuses on a single year in the course of which "Shakespeare completed *Henry the Fifth*, wrote *Julius Caesar* and *As You Like It* in quick succession, then drafted *Hamlet*" (xi). Shapiro's "surgical incisions into a single year, coupled with a poignant sense of social tension and injustices, show that context is all" (Haven, n. pag.) Indeed, confining the narrative to a single year, looking at that particular period in forensic detail, and using every available information in the service of creating a context, works remarkably well in terms of the effect of much desired vividness and the sense of lived life. The narrative comes alive with scenes like this:

> As the snow fell, a dozen or so armed men gathered in Shoreditch, in London's northern suburbs. Instead of the clubs usually wielded in London's street brawls or apprentice riots, they carried deadly weapons – "swords, daggers, bills, axes and such like." Other than the Tower of London, which

> housed England's arsenal, about the only places to come by some of the larger weapons were the public theatres, where they were used to give a touch of realism to staged combat. In all likelihood, these weapons were borrowed from the Curtain playhouse, near Finsbury Field, temporary home of the Chamberlain's Men.
>
> The armed men didn't have far to go. Their destination was another playhouse in Shoreditch, the nearby Theatre. [...] Local residents seeing the armed troupe approach, may well have been confused about what was happening during this week of holiday revels, for at the head of the group was the leading tragedian in England, the charismatic star of the Chamberlain's Men, Richard Burbage. But this was no impromptu piece of street theatre. Burbage, his older brother Cuthbert, and the rest of the men bearing weapons were there in deadly earnest, about to trespass and take back what they considered rightfully theirs, and, if necessary, come to blows with anyone trying to stop them. (2)

It is usually taught that we know precious little of Shakespeare's life, but a narration such as Shapiro's makes us realize that actually he left quite a number of traces behind. It forces us to rethink our expectations from a biography. The positive answer to the question, "Is completeness desirable and necessary?" loses its strength because we see that a microscopic approach is capable of yielding quite a strong biographical impression and can be a persuasive alternative to a larger-scoped narrative.

The year 1599 was a historically fascinating year for Queen Elizabeth's realm: There was an Irish rebellion, a palpable anxiety over who would succeed the Queen, Earl of Essex's fall from favour, a threat from the Spanish armada, Edmund Spenser's death, and the unauthorized publication of *The Passionate Pilgrim*. Shapiro expresses the reason for choosing this particular year thus:

> I have chosen to write about 1599 not only because it was an unusually fraught and exciting year but also because, as critics have long recognized, it was a decisive one, perhaps *the* one, in Shakespeare's development as a writer (and happily, one from which a surprising amount of information about his professional life survives). My interest in this subject dates back fifteen years. At that time, though I was familiar with Shakespeare's plays and taught them regularly, I didn't know about the historical moment in which plays like *As You Like It* and *Hamlet* were written and which they engaged. [...] This work, then, grew out of frustration with how much I didn't know and frustration with scholars of all critical denominations who never quite got around to addressing the question I found most pressing: how, at age thirty-five, Shakespeare went from being an exceptionally talented writer to one of the greatest who ever lived. (xvi- xvii)

The decision on the biographer's part to reconstruct one pivotal year from Shakespeare's life does away with the illusion that a life can be reconstructed in its entirety. In Shapiro's opinion it also does away with a wrong assumption:

> [...] Cradle-to-grave biographers of Shakespeare tend to assume that what makes people who they are now, made people who they were then. Historians of sixteenth-century England are not so sure. Because almost nobody thought to write a memoir or keep a personal diary in Shakespeare's day – revealing enough facts in themselves – we don't know whether their emotional lives were like ours. Their formative years certainly weren't. (xv)

This might suggest that this micro-historical alternative might work best with subjects who did not leave a great deal of personal documents behind. In the absence of the substantial support of diaries, letters, memoires etc. (such as Holroyd had at his disposal while writing Strachey's life), a sound method could be to illuminate one particular moment in the subject's personal history. As Gary Taylor says, "Shapiro's focus on a single year lets him linger on [the] textured surface details of a life more real and revealing than the grand, breathless fictions that fill out most biographies of Shakespeare."

Charles Nicholl's *The Lodger Shakespeare: His Life on Silver Street* (2007) engages with its subject in a similar way. True to the epigraph that precedes the narrative ("Ever contact leaves traces ..." Edmond Locard, *Manuel de Technique Policière*, 1923), this biographical work creates a subtle and intimate atmosphere. The starting point of the story itself carries the quiet thrill of the unassuming, ordinary, yet deeply moving trace of physical presence. Shakespeare's signature under his deposition in a lawsuit, dated Monday, 11 May 1612.

> The signature draws the eye. It is, as the graphologists say, a "frozen gesture"; it touches this otherwise unlovely piece of paper with Shakespeare's physical presence. But what makes this document special is not just – not even primarily – the signature. It is the anonymously scripted text above it, the text which the signature authenticates as Shakespeare's sworn statement. We know the thousands of lines he wrote in plays and poems, but this is the only occasion when his actual spoken words are recorded. (3)

Starting with this elegantly expressed clue, Nicholl shows the connection between the plaintiff, the defendant and Shakespeare and goes on "to look into some aspects of Shakespeare's life in London over a couple of years in the early seventeenth century" (xvii).

During these "couple of years" Shakespeare was the lodger of Christopher and Marie Mountjoy, living in an upstairs room over Mountjoy's workshop on Silver Street, Cripplegate. How does Nicholl know this? Joan Johnson, Mountjoy's maidservant who was present in the court room that day and gave her deposition alongside Shakespeare refers to "one Mr Shakespeare that laye in the house" (5) which meant in Elizabethan and Jacobean usage that he stayed there as a lodger . This simple statement of the maidservant, the phrase that was uttered by an ordinary person who knew William Shakespeare as part of her everyday existence suddenly makes him surprisingly real. Nicholl explains:

> "One Mr Shakespeare ..." I think it was the marvellous banality of this phrase that first sparked my interest in the case. For a moment we see him not from the viewpoint of literary greatness, but as he was seen by the maid of the house, a woman of no literary pretensions, indeed unable to sign her name except with a rather quavery little mark. "Mr" is perhaps not quite as banal as it looks, because it was at that time a contraction of "Master" rather than of "Mister" – it is the term of address for a gentleman, a connotation of status. But the effect is the same. We have a fleeting sense of Shakespeare's "other" life, the daily, ordinary (or ordinary-seeming) life which we know so little. He is merely the lodger, the gent in the upstairs chamber: a certain Mr Shakespeare. (6)

Here lies the core of this particular biography. It aims to show its illustrious subject in the midst of his daily life – the noise and bustle of London that envelops him. The sense of a private life away from the theatre gives this biography its freshness and uniqueness. It works particularly well when Nicholl shows the possible alchemy through which the material from everyday life turns into art:

> Just outside the frame of our imagined engraving – involved only in a casual, non-professional sense, but involved nonetheless – is a well-dressed gentleman of middle age who might perhaps be a merchant or mercer, but who is in fact the tiremaker's lodger, 'one Mr Shakespeare'. He passes on his way to and from the street, keeping his slightly odd

> hours; he is a shadow in the doorway, a footstep on the stairs. He is familiar with the scene whose outlines I have tried to construct: he observes and enquires, and what he sees and hears is stored away in that capacious and miraculously accessible memory, to be used in turn as raw material in the manufacturing of metaphors –
>
> Thou immaterial skein of sleave-silk, thou green sarcenet flap for a sore eye, thou tassel of a prodigal's purse ... (*Troilus and Cressida*, 5. 1. 29-30)
>
> Sleep that knits up the ravell'd sleave of care ... (Macbeth, 2. 2. 36)
>
> Be't when she weav'd the sleided silk
> With fingers long, small, white as milk ... (Pericles, 4 Chor. 21-2)
>
> [...] [This last one is the] vivid image of the lost daughter Marina in *Pericles*, and her slender white fingers weaving 'sleided' (sleaved) silk [...] The image may be a memory of the Mountjoy workshop – one wonders whose pale hands he is remembering. (166-67).

Although the scope of this biographical narrative is narrow, the vividness of life it creates is powerful. At the end of a glimpse at Shakespeare's life as Mountjoys' lodger, "the characters who have populated this little corner of Shakespeare's life now slip back into the shadows briefly penetrated by the Belott – Mountjoy suit" (274), leaving behind an impression that, as a reader, one has become closer to the subject of the biography. The fact that such an approach to life-writing leaves a darkness around the illuminated space or time does not diminish the vibrancy of the scene – on the contrary, it makes the scene brighter.

The micro-historical ways of looking at the subjects employed by Shapiro and Nicholl is especially suited to subjects whose lives cannot be well-documented throughout, but present a concentration of biographical detail around certain periods, places or events. Therefore, it is not difficult to see why a biographical narrative on William Shakespeare yields such inspiring texts in both cases.

* * *

We have started our discussion on biographical distance with Jane Austen biographies, let us also conclude with one. In 2013, biographer Paula Byrne published *The Real Jane Austen: A Life in Small Things*. It coincided with the bicentenary of *Pride and Prejudice* and it employed a method which the art historian and museum director Neil MacGregor used to great effect, first in his BBC Radio 4 series *A History of the World in 100 Objects* (2010), and then, in *Shakespeare's Restless World: An Unexpected History in Twenty Objects* (2012). Byrne too picks twenty objects and tells Jane Austen's story through the personal, familial, cultural, historical and economical associations of each. Freed from the confinement of chronology, the narrative moves through these associations and this movement is outward with an object at its centre. It points to the wider, chaotic, and fascinating world which Austen inhabited – in that sense the method Byrne uses is what Peter J. Conradi describes as kaleidoscopic. This biographer wants to banish once and for all the image of Austen's life as secluded, inward looking and "uneventful" and her method fits the purpose perfectly.

Byrne suggests that there is a close connection between the details of everyday life and Austen's art:

> The "correct and striking representation" of scenes from "ordinary life", rendered with precision, tact and minute detail: this is indeed the essence of Austen's art, as it is with Dutch realism in painting. Vermeer creates the sense of a real world by means of an opened letter, a pearl earring, a latticed window, a jug and a tablecloth, a musical instrument. By the same account, objects play a key part in bringing alive Austen's fictional worlds. (9)

So, true to the artistic preferences of the subject herself, this biographical narrative will be woven around "simple things." These include an East Indian shawl which leads to the exploration of young women travelling great distances in order to find a husband, in the case of Jane Austen's aunt, to India; vellum notebooks in which Austen wrote her juvenilia explores her response to the literature of her time through irony and laughter; a card of lace takes us to Bath where another aunt was imprisoned for shoplifting and went through a trial under the possibility of being sent to Australia; a portrait of Lord Mansfield's adopted daughters leads to a section on slavery; a pair of topaz crosses opens the scene onto the Navy. The chapters put side by side, create a tapestry of Austen's life experience. Given the fact that Austen did not leave any diaries or memoirs and that only 160 of her letters survived, Byrne's method is a highly effective alternative to a traditional biography which would inevitably contain conjecture. Byrne says:

> Two hundred years on from the publication of *Sense and Sensibility,* it is time for a new direction in Austen biography. The family memoir by James Edward Austen-Leigh inaugurated the tradition of the full-length treatment. It proceeded from cradle to grave at uneventful pace and with provincial calm. Biography after biography has followed the pattern of James Edward and tracked James Austen's daily life from Steventon to Bath to Chawton to Winchester. The problem with traditional biographies of this sort is that they tend to lose sight of the wood for the trees. The biographer who seeks to tell the full story has a duty to cover every base, to treat each aspect of the life with equal weight. The essential insights are often buried amidst the incidental facts. […]
> My own attempt [...] seeks to avoid the deadening march from cradle to grave by focusing each chapter on a key moment, represented by a variety of vivid scenes and objects in

> the life and work. Each moment will lead into an account of both a phase of Austen's life and a key aspect of her novels. (Afterword, n. pag.)

Sir Walter Scott, the greatly admired novelist and poet of his age envied Austen her ability to create a sense of realism. On 14 March 1826, he wrote the following in his diary:

> Also read again, and for the third time at least, Miss Austen's very finely written novel of *Pride and Prejudice*. That young lady had a talent for describing the involvements and feelings and characters of ordinary life, which is to me the most wonderful I ever met with. The Big Bow-wow stain I can do myself like any now going; but the exquisite touch, which renders ordinary commonplace things and characters interesting, from the truth of description and sentiment, is denied to me. What a pity such a gifted creature died so early.

Byrne's alternative biography is deeply rooted in the everyday reality of things – Austen would have approved.

* * *

Now as always biographers are walking in the footsteps of their subjects, they are searching for facts, reaching for the elusive, and finding new ways to create a living, breathing human being out of words. As the recent, highly public dispute between scholar/biographer Jonathan Bate and Ted Hughes Estate showed us, life-writing is still an intricate endeavour, and the biographer – subject dynamic fascinating to observe.

So, are meta-biography and other alternative forms of life-writing going to replace straight forward biography? The traditional biography is a tough act to follow. It has been one of the highest selling genres for decades. Will readers be willing to give up a seamlessly told, "complete" story or the lure of letters, diaries, anecdotes; the charm of a single minded, infinitely passionate, and even obsessive biographer for the darker charms of the behind the scenes look at the genre? In an article published at the turn of the twenty-first century, Jackie Wullschlager writes:

> Biography is a reactionary form. It comes out of the human need to make heroes and to make sense of history through individuals; it thrives on straightforward narrative, combined, in the best examples, with critical insight and scholarly apparatus. It is strong in Anglo-Saxon culture, with its empirical roots, and it is no coincidence that its exceptional popularity has coincided with the decline in the traditional plot-and-character novel, for which to some extent it has become a substitute. Although its research and intellectual vigour link it to academic criticism, it withstood structuralism and Marxism and will outlast post-modernism too. (7)

It seems biography has already found new and interesting ways to outlast any -ism. At its heart, this genre is actually a manifestation of the individual's need to make sense of himself/herself. This is the shared quest of the biographer and the reader – together they watch another individual on a quest of his/her own, and that is always a fascinating experience. After all, who really cares about the elusiveness of what one is searching for? It is the quest that counts.

Bibliography

Aaron, Daniel, ed. *Studies in Biography*. Cambridge: Harvard University Press, 1978.

Alexander, Paul. *Rough Magic: A Biography of Sylvia Plath*. New York: Da Capo Press, 2003.

Alpers, Antony. "Biography – The Scarlet Experiment." *The Literary Biography: Problems and Solutions*. Ed. Dale Salwak. London: Macmillan, 1996. 12-21.

Altick, Richard D. *Lives and Letters: A History of Literary Biography in England and America*. New York: Alfred A. Knopf. 1966.

Atlas, James. "The Biographer and the Murderer." *New York Times Magazine*, 12 Dec. 1993: 74-75.

Austen, Henry. "Biographical Notice of the Author." *Persuasion*. Ed. D. W. Harding. London: Penguin, 1985.

Austen-Leigh, William, and Richard Arthur Austen-Leigh. *Jane Austen, Her Life and Letters, a Family Record*. London: Smith, Elder & Co., 1913.

Austen-Leigh, William, and Richard Arthur Austen-Leigh. *Jane Austen, a family record*. Rev. ed. Deirdre Le Faye. Boston: G. K. Hall, 1989.

Backscheider, Paula R. *Reflections on Biography*. New York: Oxford University Press, 1999.

Bacon, Francis. *The Advancement of Learning*. Ed. Joseph Devey. New York: Collier & Sons, 1902.

Bailey, David. "Charms and the Man (Michael Holroyd)." *Vanity Fair* Sept. 1991: 215-42.

Baron Samuel H., and Carl Pletsch, eds. *Introspection in Biography*. North Carolina: The Analytic Press, 1985.

Batchelor, John, ed. *The Art of Literary Biography*. Oxford: Clarendon Press, 1995.

Bate, Walter Jackson. *Samuel Johnson*. London: Hogarth Press, 1984.

Bertaux, Daniel, ed. *Biography and Society: The Life History Approach to Social Sciences*. New York: Sage, 1981.

Booth, Wayne C. *The Rhetoric of Fiction.* 2nd ed. Chicago: Chicago University Press, 1983.

Boswell, James. *Life of Johnson*. Ed. R. W .Chapman. Oxford: Oxford University Press, 1980.

—. *Journal of the Tour to the Hebrides with Samuel Johnson LL.D. With Johnson's Journey to the Western Islands of Scotland*. Ed. R. W. Chapman. London and New York: Oxford University Press, 1979.

—. *The Correspondence and Other Papers of James Boswell Relating to the Making of the Life of Johnson.* Ed. Marshall Waingrow. Vol. 2. *The Yale Edition of the Private Papers of James Boswell*, 5 vols. New York: McGill, 1950-1959.

Bowen, Catherine D. *Biography: The Craft and the Calling*. Boston: Little, Brown, 1969.

Brack, O. M., and Robert E. Kelley, eds. *The Early Biographies of Samuel Johnson*. Iowa: University of Iowa Press, 1974.

Braithwaite, Rudolph. "Samuel Johnson's *Life of Savage* and the Language of Reprieve". *College Language Association Journal* 28.3 (1985): 344-53.

Bromwich, David. "The Uses of Biography". *Yale Review* 73 (1984): 161-75.

Broughton, Trev Lynn. *Men of Letters, Writing Lives*. New York: Routledge, 1999.

Browning, John, ed. *Biography in the Eighteenth Century*. New York: Garland, 1980.

Butt, John. *Biography in the Hands of Walton, Johnson and Boswell*. Los Angeles, 1966.

Butscher, Edward. *Sylvia Plath: Method and Madness.* Tuscon: Schaffner Press, 2003.

Byrne, Paula. "Afterword." *Persuasions On-Line* 32. 2 (2012): n. pag. Web. 30 Nov. 2014.

—. *The Real Jane Austen*. New York: Harper Collins, 2013.

Conradi, Peter J. "Not-So-Quiet Jane". *Times Literary Supplement*. 1 May 2013. Web. 30 Nov. 2014.

Cecil, David. *A Portrait of Jane Austen*. New York: Hill and Wang, 1978.

Chapman, R. W., ed. *Jane Austen: Selected Letters*. Oxford: Oxford University Press, 1985.

Clifford, James L. *From Puzzles to Portraits: Problems of a Literary Biographer*. Chapel Hill: University of North Carolina Press, 1970.

—. *Biography as an Art: Selected Criticism 1560-1960*. New York: Oxford University Press, 1962.

Clingham, G. *New Light on Boswell*. London: Cambridge University Press, 1991.

Cockshut, A. O. J. *Truth to Life: The Art of Biography in the Nineteenth Century*. London: Colliers, 1974.

Daghlian, Philip B., ed. *Essays in Eighteenth Century Biography*. Bloomingdale: Indiana University Press, 1968.

Donaldson, Ian, Peter Read, and James Walter, eds. *Shaping Lives: Reflections on Biography*. Canberra: Humanities Research Center, 1992.

Durling, Dwight, and William Watt, eds. *Biography: Varieties and Parallels*. New York: Dryden Press, 1941.

Eakin, Paul J. *The Ethics of Life Writing*. New York: Cornell University Press, 2004.

Edel, Leon. *Literary Biography*. Toronto: Toronto University Press, 1957.

—. "The Poetics of Biography". *Contemporary Approaches to English Studies*, Ed. Hilda Schiff. London: Heinemann, 1977. 38-58.

—. *Writing Lives: Principia Biographica*. New York: Norton, 1984.

__. Introductory note. *Eminent Victorians*. By Lytton Strachey. i.

Edmonds, Michael. *Lytton Strachey: A Bibliography*. New York: Garland Publishers, 1981.

Ellis, David. *Literary Lives: Biography and the Search for Understanding*. Edinburgh: Edinburgh University Press, 2000.

Ellmann, Richard. *Golden Codgers: Biographical Speculations*. New York: Oxford University Press, 1973.

—. *Literary Biography*. London: Oxford University Press, 1971.

Empson, William. *Using Biography*. London: Chatto & Windus, 1984.

Epstein, William. *Contesting the Subject: Essays in the Postmodern Theory and Practice of Biography and Biographical Criticism*. Indiana: Indiana University Press, 1991.

—. *Recognizing Biography*. Philadelphia: University of Pennsylvania Press, 1987.

Friedson, Anthony M. *New Directions in Biography*. Biography Research Center: University Press of Hawaii, 1981.

France, Peter, and William St Claire, eds. *Mapping Lives: The Uses of Biography*. London: British Academy and Oxford University Press, 2002.

Garraty, John A. *Nature of Biography*. New York: Knopf, 1957.

Gaskell, Elizabeth. *The Life of Charlotte Brontë*. London: Penguin, 1985.

Gillies, Midge. *Writing Lives: Literary Biography*. Cambridge: Cambridge University Press, 2009.

Gittings, Robert. *Nature of Biography*. Seattle: University of Washington Press, 1978.

Gould, W., and T. E. Stanley, eds. *Writing the Lives of Writers*. New York: Macmillan Press, 1998.

Halperin, John. *The Life of Jane Austen*. Baltimore: Johns Hopkins University Press, 1986.

Hamilton, Ian. *Keepers of the Flame: Literary Estates and the Rise of Biography*. London: Pimlico, 1993.

Hamilton, Nigel. *Biography: A Brief History*. Cambridge: Harvard University Press, 2007.

Haven, Cynthia L. "Will in the World". *Washington Post.* 18 Dec. 2005. Web. 20 Jan. 2015.

Hawkins, John. *Life of Samuel Johnson (1787)*. Ed. and abr. Bertram H. Davis. London: Jonathan Cape, 1962.

Hayman, Ronald. *The Death and Life of Sylvia Plath*. Stroud: Sutton Publishing, 2003.

Heilbrun, Carolyn G. *Writing a Woman's Life*. New York: Norton, 1988.

Hibbard, Allen. "Biographer and Subject: A Tale of Two Narratives." *South Central Review*. 23. 3 (2006): 19-36.

Hoberman, Ruth. *Modernizing Lives: Experiments in English Biography, 1918-1939*. Carbondale and Edwardsville: Southern Illinois University Press, 1987.

Hodge, Jane Aiken. *Only a Novel: The Double Life of Jane Austen*. New York: Coward, McCann & Geoghegan, Inc., 1972.

Holmes, Richard. *Dr Johnson and Mr Savage*. New York: Vintage, 1994.

—. *Footsteps: Adventures of a Romantic Biographer*. London: Vintage, 1996.

Holroyd, Michael. *Lytton Strachey: The New Biography*. New York: Farrar, Straus and Giroux, 1995.

—. *Works on Paper: The Craft of Biography and Autobiography*. Boston: Little, Brown, 2002.

Honan, Park. *Author's Lives: On Literary Biography and the Arts of Language*. New York: St. Martin's Press, 1990.

—. *Jane Austen, Her Life*. New York: St. Martin's Press, 1989.

—. *Shakespeare: A Life*. Oxford: Oxford University Press, 1998.

Homberger, Eric, and John Charmley, eds. *The Troubled Face of Biography*. New York: St. Martin's Press, 1988.

Hyde, Marietta, ed. *Modern Biography*. New York: Harcourt, Brace and Company, 1926.

Jenkins, Elizabeth. *Jane Austen*. London: First Sphere Books, 1972.

Johnson, Edgar. *One Mighty Torrent: The Drama of Biography.* 2nd ed. New York: Macmillan, 1955.

Johnson, Samuel. "The Life of Savage." *Samuel Johnson: Rasselas, Poems and Selected Prose.* Ed. Bertrand H. Bronson. New York: Holt, Reinhart and Winston, 1971. 500-86.

—. *The Idler and The Adventurer*. Ed. W. J. Bates, J. M. Bullitt and L. F. Powell. New Haven and London: Yale University Press, 1963.

—. *Selected Writings*. Ed. Peter Martin. Cambridge: Harvard University Press, 2011.

Jones, Charles. *Saints' Lives and Chronicles in Early England*. Ithaca, NY: Cornell University Press, 1947.

Kendall, Paul Murray. *The Art of Biography*. New York: Norton, 1965.

Le Faye, Deirdre., ed. *Jane Austen's Letters.* 3rd ed. Oxford: Oxford University Press, 1997.

—. "Memoirs and Biographies." *Jane Austen in Context*. Ed. Janet Todd. Cambridge: Cambridge University Press, 2007. 51-58.

Lee, Hermione. *Body Parts: Essays in Life-Writing*. London: Chatto & Windus, 2005.

—. *Biography: A Very Short Introduction*. Oxford: Oxford University Press, 2009.

Lee, Sidney. *Principles of Biography*. Cambridge: Cambridge University Press, 1911.

—. *The Perspective of Biography*. Cambridge: Cambridge University Press, 1918.

Longaher, John Mark. *Contemporary Biography*. Philadelphia: University of Pennsylvania Press, 1934.

MacGregor, Neil. *A History of the World in 100 Objects.* London: Penguin, 2012.

—. *Shakespeare's Restless World: An Unexpected History in Twenty Objects*. London: Penguin, 2014.

Malcolm, Janet. *The Silent Woman*. London: Papermace, 1995.

Marcus, Laura. *Auto/Biographical Discourses: Theory, Criticism, Practice.* Manchester: Manchester University Press, 1994.

Matthews, William, and Ralph Rader. *Autobiography, Biography, and the Novel.* Los Angeles: William Andrews Clark Memorial Library, University of California, 1973.

Maurois, André. *Aspects of Biography*. New York: D. Appleton & Co. 1930.

Mayer T. F. and D. R. Woolf. *The Rhetorics of Life Writing in Early Modern Europe*. Michigan: The University of Michigan Press, 1995.

Meyers, Jeffrey, ed. *The Craft of Literary Biography*. London: Macmillan, 1985.

Miller, Lucasta. *The Brontë Myth.* New York: Anchor, 2005.

Motion, Andrew. *Keats*. Chicago: University of Chicago Press, 1999.

Nadel, Ira Bruce. *Fiction, Fact and Form*. New York: St. Martin's Press, 1984.

Nicholl, Charles. *The Lodger Shakespeare: His Life on Silver Street*. New York: Viking, 2008.

Nicolson, Harold. *The Development of English Biography*. New York: Harcourt, Brace, 1928.

Nokes, David. *Samuel Johnson: A Life*. London: Faber, 2010.

—. *Jane Austen: A Life*. London: Fourth Estate, 1997.

Noonan, James, ed. *Biography and Autobiography*. Ottawa: Carleton University Press, 1993.

Novarr, David. *The Lines of Life: Theories of Biography, 1880-1970*. West Lafayette: Purdue University Press, 1986.

O'Connor, Ulick. *Biographers and the Art of Biography*. London: Quartet Books, 1991.

Oates, Stephen B. *Biography as High Adventure: Life Writers Speak on Their Art*. Amherst: University of Massachusetts Press, 1986.

Pachter Marc. *Telling Lives: The Biographer's Art*. Washington D.C.: New Republic Books and National Portrait Gallery, 1979.

Parke, Catherine Neal. *Biography: Writing Lives*. New York: Twayne Publishers, 1996.

—. *Samuel Johnson and Biographical Thinking*. Missouri: Missouri University Press, 1990.

Parker, Keiko. "Sense and 'Non-Sense' in Eight Jane Austen Biographies." *Persuasions* 12 (1989): 24-33.

Pinto, Vivian de Sola. *English Biography in the Seventeenth Century*. London: Harrap, 1951.

Plutarch. *Makers of Rome: Nine Lives*. London: Penguin Books, 1965.

Piozzi, Hester Lynch, and William Shaw. *Memoirs of the Life and Writings of the Late Dr. Samuel Johnson and Anecdotes of the Late Samuel Johnson, L.L.D. During the Last Twenty Years of His Life*. Ed. Arthur Sherbo. London: Oxford University Press, 1974.

Reed, Joseph W. *English Biography in the Early Nineteenth Century, 1801-1838*. New Haven: Yale University Press, 1966.

Redford, Bruce. *Designing the Life of Johnson*. Oxford: Oxford University Press, 2002.

Rogers, Pat. Introduction. *Life of Johnson*. By James Boswell. Oxford: Oxford University Press, 1980. v-xxxiv.

Rollyson, Carl. *Biography: An Annotated Bibliography*. Macgill Bibliographical Series. Pasadena, California: Salem Press, 1992.

Rose, Jacqueline. *The Haunting of Sylvia Plath*. London: Virago, 2014.

Rushdie, Salman. *Midnight's Children*. London: Penguin, 1991.

Sambrook, James. *James Thomson (1700-1748): A Life*. Oxford: Oxford University Press, 1991.

Sardica, Jose Miguel. "The Content and Form of 'Conventional' Historical Biography." *Rethinking History: The Journal of Theory and Practice* 17. 3 (2003): 383-400.

Scherwatzky, Steven D. "Complicated Virtue: The Politics of Samuel Johnson's *Life of Savage*." *Eighteenth Century Life* 25.3 (2001): 80-93.

Schoenbaum, S. *Shakespeare's Lives*. Oxford: Clarendon Press, 1991.

Scott, Sir Walter. *The Journal of Sir Walter Scott*. Ed. J. G. Tait. Edinburgh: Oliver & Boyd, 1939.

Selwak, Dale, ed. *The Literary Biography: Problems and Solutions.* London: Macmillan, 1996.

Shakespeare, William. *The Merchant of Venice.* London: Arden, 1964.

Shapiro, James. *A Year in the Life of William Shakespeare: 1599.* New York: Harper Perennial, 2006.

—. "Silken Threads and Silences." *Guardian*. 27 Oct. 2007. Web. 10 Feb. 2015.

Shelston, Alan. *Biography*. London: Methuen, 1977.

Showalter, Elaine. "Going Underground". *London Review of Books*. 12 May 1994: 3-5.

Sisman, Adam. *Boswell's Presumptuous Task: The Making of The Life of Dr Johnson*. New York: Farrar, Straus & Giroux, 2001.

Spurr, Barry. *A Literary-Critical Analysis of the Complete Prose Works of Lytton Strachey: A Re-Assessment of His Achievement and Career*. New York: E. Mellen Press, 1995.

Stauffer, Donald Alfred. *The Art of Biography in Eighteenth-Century England.* 2 vols. Princeton: Princeton University Press, 1941.

—. *The English Biography before 1700*. New York: Russell & Russell, 1964.

Stephen, Leslie. "National Biography". *Studies of a Biographer*. Vol. 1. London: Duckworth & Co., 1898.

Stevenson, Anne. *Bitter Fame: A Life of Sylvia Plath.* Boston: Mariner Books, 1998.

Strachey, Lytton. *Eminent Victorians*. London: Penguin, 1986.

—. *Portraits in Miniature and Other Essays*. New York: Harcourt, Brace & World, 1931.

—. *Spectatorial Essays.* "A New History of Rome." New York: Harcourt, Brace, 1965.

Stuart, Duane Reed. *Epochs of Greek and Roman Biography*. New York: Biblo and Tannen, 1967.

Suchoff, David, and Mary Rhiel, eds. *The Seductions of Biography*. New York: Routledge, 1996.

Sutherland, Kathryn. "Jane Austen's Life and Letters." *A Companion to Jane Austen*. Ed. Claudia L. Johnson and Clara Tuite. Oxford: Wiley-Blackwell, 2009. 13-30.

Taylor, Gary. "The Bard Goes Global". *Guardian*. 4 June 2005. Web. 11 Apr. 2015.

Tekcan, Rana. "Too Far For Comfort? A Discussion of Narrative Strategies in Biography." *Life Writing: Autobiography, Biography, and Travel Writing in Contemporary Literature*. Ed. Koray Melikoğlu. Stuttgart, Germany: Ibidem-Verlag, 2007. 47-65.

—. "Getting to Know Miss Jane Austen: Images of an Author." *Global Jane Austen*. New York: Palgrave Macmillan, 2013. 255-69.

Thayer, William Roscoe. *The Art of Biography*. New York: Charles Scribner's Sons, 1920.

Tonkin, Boyd. "Charles Nicholl: Low Life, High Art". *Independent*. 2 Nov. 2007. Web. 10 Feb. 2015.

Tomalin, Claire. *Jane Austen: A Life*. New York: Alfred A. Knopf, 1998.

Tracy, Clarence. *The Artificial Bastard: A Biography of Richard Savage*. Toronto: Toronto University Press, 1953.

Vance, John A. *Boswell's Life of Johnson: New Questions, New Answers*. Athens, GA: University of Georgia Press, 1985.

Wagner-Martin, Linda. *Telling Women's Lives: The New Biography*. New York: Rutgers University Press, 1994.

Wendorf, Richard. *The Elements of Life: Biography and Portrait Painting in Stuart and Georgian England*. Oxford: Oxford University Press, 1990.

Whittemore, Reed. *Pure Lives: The Early Biographers*. Baltimore: Johns Hopkins University Press, 1988.

—. *Whole Lives: Shapers of Modern Biography*. Baltimore: Johns Hopkins University Press, 1989.

Wood, Gaby. "Devil in the Detail: Janet Malcolm Interview". *Telegraph.* 29 July 2013. Web. 12 May 2015.

Woolf, Virginia. "The Art of Biography." *Collected Essays*. Ed. Leonard Woolf. Vol. 4. New York: Harcourt, Brace & World, 1967. 221-28.

—. "The New Biography." *Collected Essays*. Ed. Leonard Woolf. Vol. 4. New York: Harcourt, Brace & World, 1967. 229-235.

Wullschlager, Jackie. "Yorkshire Bodice-Ripper." Rev. of *The Brontë Myth,* by Lucasta Miller. *Financial Times Weekend* 20-21 Jan. 2001: 7.

Index

Abbey, Richard, 134, 135
Abbey School, 122
Abotsholme School, 101
Addison, Joseph, 13
Alpers, Anthony, 8, 9, 11
Antonelli, Cardinal, 76
Apostles, the (Cambridge Conversazione Society), 105, 106
Arnold, Matthew, 113
Arnold, Dr. Thomas 70, 72, 82-86, 101, 145
Augustus, John, 90
Austen, Caroline, 125
Austen, Cassandra, 1, 5, 6, 120, 122, 125-28
Austen, Cassandra Leigh, 122
Austen, Edward, 128, 129
Austen, Frank, 117-21
Austen, George Reverend, 120, 122, 129
Austen, Henry, 2, 6
  "Biographical Notice of the Author", 2
Austen, James, 6, 127
Austen, Jane, 1-7, 52, 113-29
  Emma, 52, 119
  Juvenilia, 122
  Mansfield Park, 6, 10, 123, 127
  Northanger Abbey, 2, 123, 126
  Persuasion, 2
  Pride and Prejudice, 3, 5, 119, 125
  Sanditon, 127
  Sense and Sensibility, 127
Austen-Leigh, Richard Arthur, 2
Austen-Leigh, William, 2
  Jane Austen, Her Life and Letters, A Family Record, 2, 115

Barnabo, Cardinal, 76
Bate, Walter Jackson, 15
Bell, Clive, 91, 105
Bigg-Wither, Alethea, 125
Bigg-Wither, Catherine, 125
Bigg-Wither, Harris, 5, 125, 126
Bigg-Wither, Lovelace, 125
Bigg-Wither, Reginald, 125
biographical distance, 8, 11, 46, 67, 89, 113, 115, 145, 146
biographical form, 8, 23, 143
biographical illusion, 8, 30, 143
Booth, Wayne C., 42
Bloomsberries, the; *see* Bloomsbury Group
Bloomsbury Group, 91-98, 107, 109, 110, 146, 147
Boswell, James, 11, 12, 16, 17, 18, 21n, 23, 25, 26, 45, 47-68, 107, 134, 143, 144, 149
  Account of Corsica, 48
  Journal of the Tour to the Hebrides, 23, 48, 49, 50, 55
  Life of Johnson, 12, 47-68, 134, 144
Brawne, Fanny, 138, 139, 140
Brontë, Anne, 150
Brontë, Charlotte, 150
Brontë, Emily, 150
Brooke, Rupert, 105
Browning, Robert, 11, 113
Burke, Edmund, 49, 66
Burney, Fanny, 53n
Byng, John, 67
Byrne, Paula, 161, 162

"Afterword", 161, 162
The Real Jane Austen: A Life in Small Things, 160
Byron, George Gordon Lord, 140

Cambridge University, 69, 100, 104, 105, 147
Cambridge Conversazione Society; *see* Apostles, the
Carrington, Dora 108, 110, 111
Cecil, Lord David, 4, 126
A Portrait of Jane Austen, 4
Cibber, Colley, 40
Cibber, Theophilus, 32
Lives of the Poets, 32
Clifford, James L., 57
Conradi, Peter J., 160
Crimean War, 79, 87

definitive biography, 7, 114, 133
Dryden, John, 13

Edel, Leon, 89,143
The Poetics of Biography, 143
Ellmann, Richard, 108
Golden Codgers, 108
Errington, Dr., 76

de Feuillide, Eliza, 123, 126
First World War 70, 146
Forde, Henry, 100
Forster, E. M. 105, 106

Garrick, David, 49, 62, 64
Gaskell, Elizabeth, 153
The Life of Charlotte Brontë, 153
Gentleman's Magazine, 13, 40, 44
Goldsmith, Oliver, 49
Gordon, General Charles, 70, 72, 86-88
Grant, Duncan, 107, 108
Gray, Thomas, 13,
Grub Street, 13

hagiography, 69, 74, 145
Halperin, John, 6, 7
The Life of Jane Austen, 6, 7
Hammond, Thomas, 137
Hartington, Lord, 88
Hastings, Warren, 94, 118n
Haven, Cynthia L., 154
Hawkins, Sir John, 16, 17, 25, 26, 54, 54n, 55, 60
Life of Samuel Johnson, 54
Herbert, Sidney, 80, 81
Hewlett, Dorothy, 131
Hill, Aaron, 24
Hodge, Jane Aiken, 4
Only a Novel: The Double Life of Jane Austen, 4
Holmes, Richard, 13, 16, 21n, 24, 25, 27, 32, 40, 42
Honberger, Eric, 12
The Troubled Face of Biography, 12
Holroyd, Michael, 69, 70, 71,73, 89-112, 115, 116, 130, 134, 145-49
Lytton Strachey: The New Biography, 89-112, 130, 134, 145-47
Honan, Park, 6, 113-30, 134, 136, 137, 147-49
Author's Lives: On Literary Biography and the Arts of Language, 116

Jane Austen: Her Life, 113-30, 134, 136, 137, 147, 148, 149
Hughes, Olwyn, 150
Hughes, Ted, 150
Hunt, Leigh, 131

Idler, *The*, 13, 14
immediacy, 12, 30, 56, 76, 92, 120 128, 141

Jenkins, Elizabeth, 6, 115, 124, 126
Jane Austen, 124n
Johnson, Dr Samuel, 11-68, 72, 74, 96, 107, 143, 144, 149
Life of Savage, 12-47, 96, 144
Lives of the English Poets, 13
"London", 13
Vanity of Human Wishes, *The* 13

Keats, George, 135
Keats, John, 130-41, 148, 149
"Endymion", 135
"Epistle to Charles Cowden Clark", 138
The Eve of St. Agnes, 137
"Hyperion", 137
"Lamia", 137
"O Solitude", 138
Otho, the Great, 139
Keats, Thomas, 134
Keynes, Maynard 105, 107, 108
Kingsmill, Hugh, 71, 90

Lamb, Henry, 69
Le Faye, Deirdre, 2n
Jane Austen, A Family Record, 2
Lefroy, Anna, 122, 123, 126
Lefroy, Fanny, 126
Lefroy, Tom, 124
Lemberts, The, 113
Literary Club, *The*, 48, 49, 54, 54n
Livy, 73
Lowell, Amy, 131

MacCarthy, Desmond, 105
Macclesfield, Anne, Countess of, (later Mrs Brett), 14, 16, 19, 36, 37
Macclesfield, Earl of, 19
MacGregor, Neil, 160
A History of the World in 100 Objects, 160
Shakespeare's Restless World: An Unexpected History in Twenty Objects, 160
Malcolm, Janet, 150
The Silent Woman, 150
Malone, Edmond, 49, 67
Manning, Henry Cardinal, 70, 72, 74-78
Marlowe, Christopher, 113
meta-biography, 133, 149, 150
Miller, James, 38
Miller, Lucasta, 150
The Brontë Myth, 150
Milnes, Richard Monckton, 132
Milton, John, 13
Montagu, Lady Mary Wortley, 29
Moore, G. E., 105
Morrell, Lady Ottoline, 70
Motion, Andrew, 113, 129, 130-41, 143, 147-49
Philip Larkin: A Writer's Life, 130
Keats, 113, 129, 130-41, 148, 149

narrative strategies, 7, 8, 9, 113, 143
Newman, Cardinal, 75, 76, 80
Nicholl, Charles, 157
The Lodger Shakespeare: His Life on Silver Street, 157
Nicolson, Harold, 52, 94, 98, 146
Nicolson, Nigel, 97, 98
Portrait of a Marriage, 98
Nightingale, Florence, 70, 72, 78-82
Suggestions for Thought to the Searchers after Truth among the Artisans of England, 81

objectivity, 9, 11, 42, 97, 98, 138, 144
Oldfield, Anne, 32
Oxford University, 51, 58, 83
Oxford Movement, 70n, 83

Paoli, General Pasquale, 65
Partridge, Frances, 94, 110, 111, 146
Partridge, Ralph, 110, 111
Percy, Bishop, 62
Plath Estate, 150
Plath, Sylvia, 150
Poe, Edgar Allen, 45
Pope, Alexander, 13, 34, 41, 83
The Dunciad, 34
Porter, Elizabeth Jervis, 59

Prince Regent, The, 2n
Rambler, *The*, 13, 14, 30, 56
Reisach, Cardinal, 76
Reynolds, Sir Joshua, 45, 46, 48, 49
Rivers, Richard Savage 4th Earl, 14, 16, 19, 20
Royal Academy, 117
Rugby School, 82, 83, 84, 86
Russell, Bertrand, 89, 94, 105

Sackville-West, Vita, 98
Savage, Richard, 11-47, 144
A Miscellany of Poems, 29
"The Author to be Let", 22, 29
"The Bastard", 29, 37
"On Public Spirit, with Regards to Public Works", 31
"The Wanderer", 22, 23, 25, 27, 29
Scott, Sir Walter, 162
The Journal of Sir Walter Scott, 162
Severn, Joseph, 133, 140
Sexual Offenses Act, 95
Shakespeare, William, 13, 85, 113, 116n
Shapiro, James, 154, 155, 156, 157, 159
A Year in the Life of William Shakespeare: 1599, 154, 156, 157
Sharp, Anne, 7
Shaw, Bernard, 90
Showalter, Elaine, 152
Shelley, Percy Bysshe, 11, 131, 140
Sheppard, John, 104
Sinclair, James, 36
Spectator, *The*, 98
Steele, Sir Richard, 31, 34, 64
Stephen, Leslie, 143
Stephen, Venessa (later Venessa Bell), 105
Stephen, Virginia; *see* Woolf, Virginia
Strachey, Alix, 69, 92, 98
Strachey, James, 91-97, 114, 115, 146,

Strachey, Lytton, 69-89, 90-112, 145, 146, 151
  Elizabeth and Essex, 69, 94
  Eminent Victorians 69-89, 98, 101, 108, 110, 112, 145, 147, 149
  Portraits in Miniature, 69
  Queen Victoria, 69
Strachey, Pippa, 110
Strachey, Richard Sir, 70, 99
Strauss, David, 84
  Das Leben Jesu, 84
Swift, Jonathan, 13

Taylor, John, 56
Thomson, James, 33
Thrale, Hester Lynch, 55, 56
  Anecdotes of the Late Samuel Johnson, 55
Thrale, Henry, 55
  Tom Brown's School Days, 83
Tomalin, Claire, 113
Tracy, Clarence, 25
Trevelyan, G. M., 68
Tyrconnel, Lord, 34

Victorianism, 70, 71, 89, 99, 145-47
Voltaire (François Marie Arouet), 73

Wilde, Oscar, 69, 94
Wilkes, John, 65, 66
Wilks, Robert, 32
Willams, Blanche, 131
Wittgenstein, Ludwig, 105
Wolpole, Sir Robert, 30
Wood, Gaby, 150
Woodhouse, Richard, 140
Woolf, Leonard, 98, 105
Woolf, Virginia, 70, 95, 105
Wullschlager, Jackie, 150, 151

STUDIES IN ENGLISH LITERATURES

Edited by Koray Melikoğlu

ISSN 1614-4651

1 *Özden Sözalan*
The Staged Encounter
Contemporary Feminism and Women's Drama
2nd, revised edition
ISBN 978-3-89821-367-6

2 *Paul Fox (ed.)*
Decadences
Morality and Aesthetics in British Literature
2nd, revised and expanded edition
ISBN 978-3-89821-0623-3

3 *Daniel M. Shea*
James Joyce and the Mythology of Modernism
ISBN 978-3-89821-574-1

4 *Paul Fox and Koray Melikoğlu (eds.)*
Formal Investigations
Aesthetic Style in Late-Victorian and Edwardian Detective Fiction
2nd, revised and expanded edition
ISBN 978-3-8382-0593-9

5 *David Ellis*
Writing Home
Black Writing in Britain Since the War
ISBN 978-3-89821-591-6

6 *Wei H. Kao*
The Formation of an Irish Literary Canon in the Mid-Twentieth Century
ISBN 978-3-89821-545-9

7 *Bianca Del Villano*
Ghostly Alterities
Spectrality and Contemporary Literatures in English
2nd, revised editon
ISBN 978-3-89821-714-9

8 *Melanie Ann Hanson*
Decapitation and Disgorgement
The Female Body's Text in Early Modern English Drama and Poetry
ISBN 978-3-89821-605-5

9 *Shafquat Towheed (ed.)*
New Readings in the Literature of British India, c.1780-1947
ISBN 978-3-89821-673-9

10 *Paola Baseotto*
"Disdeining life, desiring leaue to die"
Spenser and the Psychology of Despair
ISBN 978-3-89821-567-1

11 *Annie Gagiano*
Dealing with Evils
Essays on Writing from Africa
2nd, revised and expanded edition
ISBN 978-3-8382-0687-5

12 *Thomas F. Halloran*
James Joyce: Developing Irish Identity
A Study of the Development of Postcolonial Irish Identity in the Novels of James Joyce
ISBN 978-3-89821-571-8

13 *Pablo Armellino*
Ob-scene Spaces in Australian Narrative
An Account of the Socio-topographic Construction of Space in Australian Literature
ISBN 978-3-89821-873-3

14 *Lance Weldy*
Seeking a Felicitous Space on the Frontier
The Progression of the Modern American Woman in O. E. Rölvaag, Laura Ingalls Wilder, and Willa Cather
ISBN 978-3-89821-535-0

15 *Rana Tekcan*
Too Far For Comfort
A Study on Biographical Distance
2nd, revised and expanded edition
ISBN 978-3-89821-995-2

16 *Paola Brusasco*
Writing Within/Without/About Sri Lanka
Discourses of Cartography, History and Translation in Selected Works by Michael Ondaatje and Carl Muller
ISBN 978-3-8382-0075-0

17 *Zeynep Z. Atayurt*
Excess and Embodiment in Contemporary Women's Writing
ISBN 978-3-89821-978-5

18 *Gianluca Delfino*
Time, History, and Philosophy in the Works of Wilson Harris
ISBN 978-3-8382-0265-5

19 *Taner Can*
Magical Realism in Postcolonial British Fiction: History, Nation, and Narration
ISBN 978-3-8382-0754-4

ibidem-Verlag / *ibidem* Press
Melchiorstr. 15
70439 Stuttgart
Germany

ibidem@ibidem.eu
ibidem.eu